HIKING
THE GREAT
NORTHWEST

HIKING THE GREAT NORTHWEST

Harvey Manning, Ira Spring, and Vicky Spring

Photographs by Bob and Ira Spring and Vicky Spring

The Mountaineers/Seattle

4
5 4 3 2

Published by The Mountaineers
1011 SW Klickitat Way, Seattle, Washington 98134

Published simultaneously in Canada by Douglas & McIntyre, Ltd., 1615 Venables Street, Vancouver, B.C. V5L 2H1

Published simultaneously in Great Britain by Cordee, 3a DeMontfort Street, Leicester, England, LE1 7HD

Manufactured in the United States of America

Edited by Dana Fos
Maps by Tom Kirkendall
Cover photograph: Chephran Lake in Banff National Park, Canadian Rockies
Frontispiece: Emperor Falls on Berg Lake trail, Mount Robson Provincial Park
Cover design by Elizabeth Watson
Book design by Bridget Culligan

Library of Congress Cataloging-in-Publication Data

Manning, Harvey.
    Hiking the great northwest : the 55 greatest trails in Washington, Oregon, Idaho, Montana, Wyoming, British Columbia, the Canadian Rockies, and northern California / by Harvey Manning, Ira Spring, and Vicky Spring.
        p.   cm.
    Includes index.
    ISBN 0-89886-284-1
    1. Hiking—Northwest, Pacific—Guide-books. 2. Hiking—Canadian Rockies (B.C. and Alta.)—Guide-books. 3. Hiking—British Columbia—Guide-books. 4. Northwest, Pacific—Description and travel—Guide-books. 5. Canadian Rockies (B.C. and Alta.)—Description and travel—Guide-books. 6. British Columbia—Description and travel—1981- —Guide-books. I. Spring, Ira. II. Spring, Vicky, 1953- . III. Title.
GV199.42.N69M36   1991
917.95—dc20   91-21630
                                                                              CIP

Contents

Selecting the Hikes
We Call "Great"

We, the authors, have hiked thousands of trails in America and several hundred in Europe and Asia. Few (if any) have failed to give us a degree of pleasure, if only a negative sort, such as piling up a record total of mosquito kills or watching a bear consume the party's entire supply of cookies and then going after the salami. Obviously, we've gained more positive enjoyment from some trails than others. Equally obviously, our designation of "great" reflects our biases in favor of the following (not in this or any other special order):

1. Spectacular views
2. Flower-filled alpine meadows
3. Lakes and streams
4. Ancient—or at least virgin—forests
5. Animals and birds
6. Solitude

If we've ever found a trail providing all six it escapes our memory. *Off* the trail is another matter. However, for our purposes here, sticking to the subject of official paths, a route that has the first three of our list usually will be light on animal population —and heavy on human. A route with Number 6 will likely also be good on Number 5 but more or less deficient in Numbers 1 and 2 and perhaps 3 and 4. However, a trail need not be a winner in every department to earn our rating as "great." It must, of course, excel in something—usually several things.

Some hiking areas are so rich in great hikes that choosing representative trails was like trying to decide which children to throw to the wolves. We know hikers who will plod vast distances of jungle, desert, and icecaps to add a single bird to their life list. We know others who won't stir from the city without the absolute guarantee of a panful of trout every breakfast. Needless to say, for each trail herein, another in the same region may better meet the individual's own biases.

Bull moose

Mount Victoria from Plain-of-the-Six-Glaciers trail, Banff National Park

Introduction

A devout pedestrian whose home hills are the Cascades is bitten by the urge to roam afield. She is intrigued by Montana. But impressions from photographs and magazine articles and friends' stories blur in her mind. Where should she start? Glacier National Park? Beartooths? Madison Range? The Crazies?

A New Jersey walker–scrambler decides to blow his life savings on a summer vacation in the Northwest, sampling as many wildlands as possible. Because he may not be able to return for a while, he can't afford to waste a single day on less than the best. When he gets to the Olympics, which one hike will guarantee a rich taste of the special flavor? What basin should be his prime goal in the Wind River Range? How and where can he be initiated quickly into the quintessential Canadian Rockies?

Visitors come from other continents, as overwhelmed by our natural treasures as we are by theirs. We often hear German, French, Japanese, and golly-knows spoken on our trails, and they frequently ask us (in English) what destinations we recommend.

For such situations and persons this book has been published—to provide our view of the best hiking trails in the Pacific Northwest, defined for the present purpose as north-of-Sierra California, Oregon, Washington, Idaho, Wyoming, Montana, southern British Columbia, and the west edge of Alberta. Contiguity and other factors make this "Northwest" a geographical province clearly distinguishable from the Colorado–California–Southwest region on one side, the northern British Columbia–Yukon–Alaska region on the other. Within it, however, lie as many differences as similarities.

For each of the trails presented here, photographs show the look of the country. Sketch maps give preliminary orientation. Text describes the trail and how to get there, tells if it is currently mobbed or lonesome, says what months the trail usually is sufficiently snowfree for hiking, and lists appropriate maps. For the last-minute detail needed to plan more than the briefest visit, one must look to maps and the land-managers (National Park Service, U.S. Forest Service, or other).

Being a Carefree Wanderer

In this book we have refrained from giving our opinions on what comestibles constitute a supreme wildland cuisine, the proper way to lace a boot, and whether or not there truly is a parka that keeps rain from coming in while letting perspiration breathe out. Several excellent manuals provide a wealth of factual detail on hiking and backpacking equipment and technique and a plethora of tips on how to coddle an egg and tape a blister.

We do feel compelled to name the Ten Essentials, considered by generations of wildland veterans to be mandatory for safe travel in wilderness.

1. Extra clothing—more than needed in good weather
2. Extra food—enough so something is left over at the end of the trip
3. Sunglasses—necessary for most alpine travel and indispensable on snow
4. Knife—for first aid and emergency firebuilding (making kindling)
5. Firestarter—a candle or chemical fuel for starting an emergency fire with wet wood
6. First-aid kit
7. Matches—in a waterproof container

Cascade Creek and Teewinot Mountain, Grand Teton National Park

8. Flashlight—with extra bulb and batteries
9. Map—be sure it's the right one for the trip
10. Compass—be sure to know the declination, east or west, for your hiking area

In the past decade it has become *de rigueur* to issue shrill warnings about giardiasis or "beaver fever" or, as it used to be called, the "Boy Scout trots." Though hikers who have lived with the *Giardia* critter for many thousands of wildland days and wildland creeks tend to chuckle, the horror stories spreading on the wind must be addressed. It is very simply done, and without any great fuss or expense: *Whenever in doubt* about the water, boil it 10 minutes, a treatment 100 percent effective not only against *Giardia* but also the myriad other filthy little blighters that may upset your digestion or—as with some forms of hepatitis—destroy your liver. (Even those wildlanders who claim immunity to giardiasis shudder at rumors of the new diseases being brought home to North America by jet-trekkers.) When boiling is not feasible, as during a day on the trail, use one of the several iodine treatments sold at backpacker shops. Chlorine compounds are untrustworthy in wildland conditions. The technology of filters is advancing, but the cost of any device worth even the least utility is high and the dependability of every one is a matter of controversy. Don't bet your liver on them.

As for other menaces—ticks (carriers of Rocky Mountain spotted fever and Lyme disease), grizzly bears, rattlesnakes, poison oak and ivy, trailhead burglars, falling off cliffs, and drowning—we leave the likes of these to the backpack manuals and the information sheets provided by local land-managers.

We would like to offer comments on adjusting to certain unfamiliar conditions. Hikers trained in the Sierra and Southwest are appalled to discover that in many northern ranges there can be rain, in volume, for days or weeks at a time; the concept of "rain gear" is novel to them. Hikers experienced in lowland travel anywhere on the continent learn to their chagrin that in the alpine elevations of northern ranges there can be snowstorms any day of summer; they are surprised that cotton shorts and T-shirts are the typical costume of hypothermia. Another shock is that in the high elevations the winter snows stay late, summer may not start until late July, and some years may have no summer whatsoever. Hikers from the coastal ranges are astounded and terrified by the horrific thunderstorms that seem to brew up on the Grand Teton every August afternoon at teatime.

Aside from regional idiosyncrasies of weather, there are peculiarities of the very air. The hiker who has spent his entire wildland career in the Cascades and Olympics, where all but a few peaks top out below 8000 feet and most camps are under 6000 feet, sets out at his normal pace to explore a tundra basin of the Wind Rivers and is alarmed to find himself gasping for breath and losing his appetite, symptoms previously unknown to him except while nearing the 14,410-foot summit of Mt. Rainier. At length he realizes that even meadow miles are substantially longer at 10,000 feet than at 5000. Indeed, he may have to spend a number of days at 2 miles high before feeling as chipper as at 1 mile and during that period of acclimatization adjust to a slower pace, deeper breathing, and modified ambitions. Finally, visitors to the higher elevations should be aware that several serious illnesses are caused by thin air. These were first identified in the Himalaya at altitudes ranging above 20,000 feet; now that the symptoms are recognized widely by medical science, they are being diagnosed at elevations of 8000 feet and even lower. It may not suffice for a victim to lay around camp a day or two; sometimes he must be immediately evacuated to lower elevations, administered oxygen, or die.

Minding Your Outdoor Manners

The bad news for our fragile wildland ecosystems is that the human population has grown so dangerously large that the old-time habits of frontiersmen cannot be tolerated. The good news is that wilderness hikers (if not every other species of traveler) of this generation have demonstrated a readiness to be educated about right and wrong and have shown a willingness—nay, an eagerness—to be good citizens. The rules of "minimum impact" are now so widely known—and so frequently repeated in manuals and in the information leaflets given out by land-managers—that they need not be stressed here, but merely remembered.

The bed (tent or tarp, ground sheet, sleeping pad, sleeping bag) must be located on tough terrain: preferably, forest duff, moraine gravel, riverbar, rock slab, or snow —never in flower gardens or heather fields.

The kitchen also must be in a durable spot and should be centered on a stove, not a wood fire; few, indeed, are the sites where wood can nowadays be used for fuel, destroying the scenery and polluting the air, and they are fewer by the year. Local land-managers tell hikers where they can burn wood and where they cannot. To be sure, wilderness travelers must know how to start a wood fire, potentially lifesaving in the wet and cold ranges of the Northwest, but they must at the same time know how to put out a fire; forests should be burned by lightning, which is a regular resident of wilderness, not man, who in the words of the National Wilderness Act is "a visitor who does not remain."

Both bed and kitchen should be placed as far from water as the terrain permits; 100 feet is the most common specification. Dishes and bodies must be washed as far as possible from streambank or lakeshore, in a place where dirt and biodegradable detergent will disperse harmlessly in the ground. By carrying a large collapsible water-carrier, trips can be minimized to the creek or lake—trips that beat down a path in precisely the most fragile soils and plants. (Such a water-carrier brings the serendipity of permitting private camps in the most crowded areas—fill up at creek or lake and clamber high on a lonesome and breezy ridge, far from mobs and mosquitoes.)

Where privies are not provided, eliminate body wastes far from watercourses. Scoop a shallow hole in forest duff or moraine gravel (not meadow grass) and bury the evidence; in this "biological disposal layer" of the ground the busy microbes will do a quick cleanup job. Do not bury toilet paper; wee creatures will dig it up for chewing and nest-making. Preferably, avoid toilet paper altogether; foliage such as the large, soft leaves of thimbleberry are very comfortable. If paper is used, carry it away in a double-layer plastic bag—the same one employed for "disposable" diapers, sanitary napkins/whatever, fish guts, and bacon grease, all of which draw nuisance visits from little critters—and dangerous visits from big bears.

Carry all garbage, every scrap, back to civilization. Where campfires are permitted, the paper may be burned en route—but never the plastic, which merely melts, nor the aluminum foil, which breaks into bits that sparkle in the ashes for thousands of years.

Do not shortcut trails, and when in meadows follow established paths—avoid those that have been closed off by rangers to restore the plantlife.

In areas of heavy population—or *any* population besides your own—do not shout or scream on the trail or stay up all night laughing and singing. You may not frighten the animals, but you will annoy folks who enjoy listening to birds and waterfalls and winds.

In summation, be clean and quiet and considerate and respectful, take only photos and leave only footprints—and these strictly on trails, rocks, or snow. Don't feed the animals and don't stomp the flowers.

Marching in the Great Crusade

Granted, the very presence of humans in a wildland—or on the Earth—is a form of pollution. No matter how far a hiker rambles, he can't get away from himself, can

Lake Solitude and the Grand Teton, Grand Teton National Park

never know *perfect* wilderness. However, so long as only a fraction of Northwest wilderness has statutory protection and the rest is wide-open to *laissez-faire* exploitation —and recreation—it is absurd to say that to walk the trails is to join the plot to destroy wilderness. Only very silly people argue for banning the publication of guidebooks in order to maximize the wilderness quality through a conspiracy of silence. Boots surely do violate virginity, but a regiment of hikers cannot equal the havoc done by three motorcycles, one jeep, or an afternoon's chainsawing. So long as there are ancient forests wanted by loggers, wild rivers wanted by dammers, and flower meadows wanted by miners, the crusade must continue to put more hikers—more defenders, more crusaders —on the fragile land.

However, we do not need more motorcycles on that land. Nor do we need their younger, quieter cousins, the rough-and-tumble knobby-tire bikes, splendid machines

Camping in Glacier Peak Wilderness

that superbly fill a large niche on city streets, rural lanes, and active or abandoned logging roads but are obscenities on the narrow, twisty trails that for generations have been the pedestrian's refuge from the mechanical ingenuities of a simian technology.

Neither do we need helicopters clattering up the wilderness sky, carrying tourists to picnic meadows, skiers to pristine powder, and climbers to "cheater" high camps. In Canada the frontier motto of "Everything Goes" still offends on a gigantic scale; American chopper jockeys do any and all damage that the Forest Service will benignly tolerate.

Most of all what we need is more land placed in national wilderness and related designations such as national parks, national wildlife refuges, national ancient forest preserves, national ecological preserves, and the like. The world is being submerged by a flood of humankind. If the species is to retain a spiritual connection with its past, there must be substantial "lifeboats" ("arks"?) where natural communities survive the deluge, helping to nurture the soul (if any exists) of man (if any remain).

Happily, many banners have been raised on high in the Great Crusade to save the Holy Land. A contemporary Peter the Hermit would echo his medieval model and preach to hikers: Fall into the line of march under any banner you choose—but do choose, and do march.

Aids to Planning and Navigation

Maps

Obviously, the first requirement for getting around the country is a set of road maps. Most American national parks and monuments and Canadian national and provincial parks offer free information leaflet-maps. With few exceptions these are helpful for broad orientation and road travel but inadequate for hiking.

Though some areas are covered by specialized, privately published maps, which are very useful, the basic tools for wilderness navigation are topographic maps, where they exist, and, where not, planimetric maps; in the United States, those are produced by the U.S. Forest Service.

TOPOGRAPHIC MAPS

To find the proper sheets for any given trip, a hiker must do a bit of homework.

United States

The U.S. Geological Survey (USGS) has prepared topographic maps for most of the nation and is working on the rest. Mountain shops and map stores often stock the sheets for their particular regions, as do information centers in national parks. However, a hiker planning to journey afar usually does best to order direct from:

Distribution Section
U.S. Geological Survey
Federal Center
Denver, Colorado 80225

First ask for an index map (free) of the desired state and then from it determine the specific sheets required. An area may be mapped in either or both of two series: the 15-minute series, on a scale of 1 inch to 1 mile; and the 7^1/$_2$-minute series, at 2^1/$_2$ inches to 1 mile.

Canada

Topographic maps for British Columbia and western Alberta may be obtained from:
Geographic Division
B.C. Lands Service
Parliament Building
Victoria, British Columbia V8V 1X4

Again, first ask for the index map. Some areas are mapped only on a rather unhelpful scale of 1 inch to 8 miles and others on a very good scale of 1 inch to 1 mile. Maps exist for all national parks (except the newest) and most provincial parks.

Canada, having recently switched to the metric system used by the whole world, except the United States and England, is a swamp of mathematical confusion for American travelers. South of the Canadian border, our directions are given in the old English system with 12 inches to 1 foot, 36 inches to 1 yard, or 5280 feet to 1 mile. North of the border, the directions are given in both the English system and in the metric with 10 centimeters to 1 meter and 1000 meters to 1 kilometer. The transition period is difficult for everyone, American and Canadian; a traveler must pay close attention because some government maps are in meters and others in feet and sometimes local people give directions in a mixture of miles and kilometers.

U.S. FOREST SERVICE

Detailed maps are available for a number of wilderness areas and sometimes are topographic; these *wilderness maps,* though not up to the high standards of the USGS, are generally the best for hiking (but not for cross-country travel). Most national forests have planimetric *forest maps* or *ranger district maps,* which lack contour lines but serve well enough—as they must for places with no other coverage. Those on a scale of $1/2$ inch to 1 mile are best.

Forest Service maps may be obtained from ranger stations, forest headquarters, and the regional headquarters listed below.

Wyoming (most of it)

U.S. Forest Service
Rocky Mountain Region 2
11177 W. Eighth Avenue
Box 25127
Lakewood, Colorado 80225

Montana (all) and Idaho

U.S. Forest Service
Northern Region 1
Federal Building
Missoula, Montana 59807

Idaho (most of it) and Wyoming (Bridger and Teton Wildernesses)

U.S. Forest Service
Intermountain Region 4
324 25th Street
Ogden, Utah 84401

Northern California
U.S. Forest Service
California Region 5
630 Sansome Street
San Francisco, California 94111

Oregon and Washington
U.S. Forest Service
Pacific Northwest Region 6
P.O. Box 3623
319 S.W. Pine Street
Portland, Oregon 97208

Rules and Regulations

The very notion of bureaucratic rules and regulations may seem antithetical to the wilderness concept, and they certainly are repugnant to those who specifically seek to

Above: *Cooling off in upper Lyman Lake.* Overleaf: *Avalanche lilies on High Divide, Mount Olympus in distance, Olympic National Park*

escape constraints of civilization. However, increases in American population and leisure time, and deterioration in the quality of urban life, have so crowded the backcountry that perfect freedom rarely is to be found anymore.

To be sure, there still are areas where one may get completely away from Big Brother. But one man's freedom is another's license, and in these "free" wildlands the hiker is likely to have his peace disturbed by jeeps, motorcycles, and "mountain" bikes, or 100-horse packtrains turning gardens into barnyards, or a regiment of hunters gunning down every creature that stirs, or a pack of yapping dogs, or helicopters flopping from the sky. Even fastidious walkers, if there are enough of them, trample flowers to dust, jam favored campsites elbow to elbow, pollute the waters, and anger the bears.

Land-managers responsible for protecting the wilderness owe their first loyalty to the land. If this sounds anti-humanistic, it must be remembered that if the land does not live, which is to say if the native plants and animals do not thrive and the waters do not remain pure, people will have no reason to go there. In the future, the freedom of the hills will be limited not only by natural law but also by human law—which hopefully will sit as lightly as possible.

The problem is relatively new in the Northwest but is worsening rapidly. Managers are seeking solutions, debating which are best, and experimenting with techniques. They do not pretend to know the final answers, which must come from trial and error, and they welcome the comments and suggestions of individual travelers.

The permit system (wilderness permit, camping permit, travel permit, fire permit, climbing permit, or whatever) is well established in most parks and many wildernesses. In some places it is presently employed solely to gather statistics; in others, to regulate the number of visitors and the trails and camps they use, even to the extent of requiring reservations made perhaps weeks or months in advance. Here and there in America a hiker actually may be barred from the trail of his choice, informed it is "full," and he must wait his turn or choose another walk.

The parks and forests are steadily deploying more backcountry and wilderness rangers who observe travel patterns and counsel visitors. In certain areas they have gone beyond the "study and advice" stage and, distasteful as it is to them, have been compelled to act as enforcers, handing out citations for illegal camping and other offenses.

Managers by and large are trying to avoid premature, officious over-control and generally are moving slowly, warily into the era of regulation. Obviously, one way to head off stricter controls, including computerized rationing, is to dedicate more parks and wilderness, and any hiker restive under restrictions surely ought to devote himself vigorously to this cause.

Meanwhile, in his wanderings through the Northwest he will encounter every degree of regulation from none at all to a rigidity that forbids him to camp where he desires, limits his stay to a specified period, requires him to abstain from wood fires, and so forth. In any given area, the rules may change from one year to the next. In at least one wilderness, permits were required in 1972 and not in 1973, it having been decided the system was not yet needed there. In at least one national park, campers were concentrated at a few designated sites to confine the damage—and after a short time this policy was junked in favor of the "scattering" technique.

The situation is so fluid the prudent hiker will want to write the appropriate land-managing agency in advance of a trip to learn the current rules and regulations; those published in a guidebook may be obsolete before the ink is dry.

The other thing the hiker can do, aside from obeying existing rules whether he likes them or not, is to comment to backcountry and wilderness rangers encountered, and by letter to superintendents of national parks and supervisors of national forests. Though their first loyalty is to the land, they want also to serve the people as best they can, and to do so they must know what the people want.

A Note About Safety

Safety is an important concern in all outdoor activities. No guidebook can alert you to every hazard or anticipate the limitations of every reader. Therefore, the descriptions of roads, trails, routes, and natural features in this book are not representations that a particular place or excursion will be safe for your party. When you follow any of the routes described in this book, you assume responsibility for your own safety. Under normal conditions, such excursions require the usual attention to traffic, road and trail conditions, weather, terrain, the capabilities of your party, and other factors. Keeping informed on current conditions and exercising common sense are the keys to a safe, enjoyable outing.

The Mountaineers

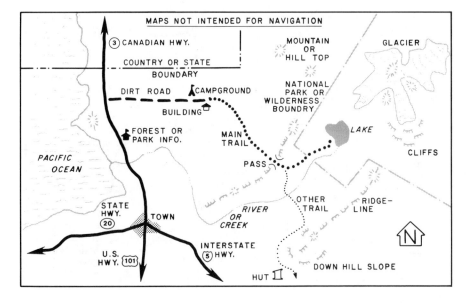

WYOMING

A person looking at a map and noting Wyoming's remoteness from the megalopolis structure of America would expect the wildlands to be virtually empty. Two factors render the situation otherwise. For one, the fault-block ranges of the Rocky Mountain Cordillera that rear up dramatically from the Great Plains are two days' drive closer to Chicago, say, than the Cascades or Sierra and, thus, for masses of Easterners, are among the easiest to reach of high mountains. For another, the scenery ranks with the finest in the West; no peak on the continent is more famous than the Grand Teton; the "gates of hell" (the geysers) in Yellowstone earned its creation as the first national park.

Still, though Wyoming suffers some of the worst tourist mobs and some of the most jamful trails, large portions of the backcountry are as purely lonesome as can be found in the old 48.

The land is high, much of it very high, and the air so thin the miles are long. Forests are generally open, broken by broad parks. Tundras glow with flowers in season. Lakes are bright in ice-scooped rock bowls. Summer weather is mainly fair except for the legendary thunderstorms, themselves worth a visit to shudder at. All in all, Wyoming is a hiker's dream.

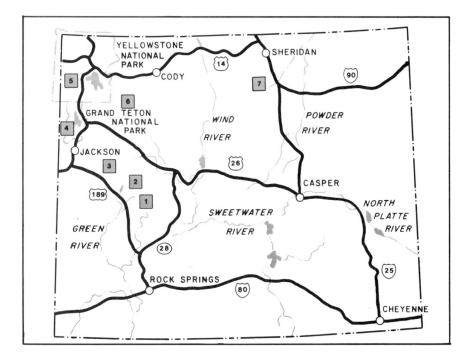

Lonesome Lake and Cirque of Towers, Wind River Range

As for climbers, they scarcely need to be told that the Tetons and Wind Rivers provide alpine tours on the best of rock, offering every degree of difficulty from simple scrambles to "experts only."

In much opinion, the Wind River Range is the greatest hiking and climbing area in the West. Protected in three wildernesses—the Fitzpatrick, Bridger, and Popo Agie—the range contains large, fairly level glaciers, rugged peaks, miles of tundra, and hundreds of lakes.

Hotfoot hikers in a hurry to "do the West" in a single summer often do a Wind River 50-mile hike in three to four days. Bad idea! The water and the meadows and the views on and off the trail—four weeks just for a start.

Lonesome Lake (Hike 1), in the southern half of the Wind River Range, and Island Lake (Hike 2), in the northern half, are just two of many great hikes.

The Gros Ventre Wilderness, a gentler, friendlier (than most, to hikers) wilderness, earns its rating as great largely because it is not well known; the scenery is not spectacular but the wildlife is, and so are the miles of alpine flower fields. The Granite Creek trail (Hike 3), has a bit of everything the wilderness has to offer.

Green Lake and Square Top Mountain, Wind River Range

While the hiking and climbing of the Wind River may be better, the Tetons are without a doubt the most famous mountains in the nation, displayed throughout the world on travel posters and in magazines and books. The roads of Grand Teton National Park are jammed by cars with license plates from every state and province in North America, along with buses crammed with tourists from around the globe. The grand scenery and the breathtaking flowers on the Lake Solitude trail (Hike 4), are well worth the overload of humankind.

Yellowstone National Park, the first national park in the world, is famous for its geysers, which all summer and even in the dead of winter are ringed by admirers. For a hiker, Yellowstone earns its great title from trails, some used more by grizzly bears than hikers and others that go to remote geysers and hot springs; the author's favorite

is Shoshone Geyser Basin on the shore of Shoshone Lake (Hike 5).

The Teton Wilderness, the least known of Wyoming's wildernesses, earns its greatness for what few other hiking areas can offer—*solitude*. Beauty is in the eyes of the beholders, some of whom rave about the miles of forest, others about the lovely rivers, the miles of meadows spread in early summer with yellow balsamroot, and the 10,000-foot peaks. All are found on the lengthy Two Ocean Pass loop (Hike 6).

The Cloud Peak Wilderness, the farthest east of Wyoming's wilderness areas, is comparatively small, yet large enough for riches of alpine lakes, glacier-sculpted mountains, and meadows of arctic flowers such as avens, moss campion, and dwarf lupine and paintbrush. The lakes are handy to roads and those with both fish and beauty are especially busy. Hike 7 traverses this wilderness.

1 • Big Sandy Lake–Lonesome Lake

DAY HIKE
Big Sandy Lake
Round trip • 12 miles
Hiking time • 6 hours
High point • 9690 feet
Elevation gain • 540 feet

BACKPACK
Lonesome Lake
Round trip • 19 miles
Hiking time • 2 days
High point • 10,600 feet
Elevation gain • 1500 feet in, 700 feet out

RESOURCES

Hikable • mid-July through September
Management • Bridger–Teton National Forest
USGS maps • Big Sandy Opening, Temple Peak, Lizard Head Peak
Hiker map • Hiking Map & Guide, Southern Wind River Range, Earthwalk Press
Information • Pinedale Ranger District, P.O. Box 220, Pinedale, Wyoming 82941;
    phone (307) 367-4326
Permits • Not needed, but camping restrictions are in force; check with the Pinedale
    Ranger Station for specifics
Protection status • Bridger and Popo Agie Wildernesses

Lonesome Lake obviously was named sometime in the dim past. Lying beneath peaks of the Cirque of Towers, it is one of the most popular destinations in the Wind Rivers, even though, unlike many other hikes in the Bridger Wilderness, it doesn't lend itself to a loop. The scenery, flowers, and lakes, more than compensating for the lack of solitude, suffice to earn greatness. The day hike follows the Big Sandy River to a lake at timberline.

Drive south of Pinedale 12 miles on US 191 and between mileposts 87 and 88

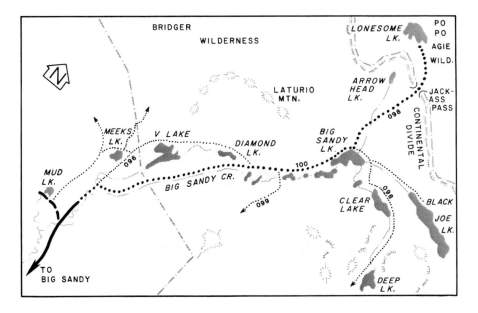

Cirque of Towers, Wind River Range

turn east to Boulder (no signs identify this turn); from there continue 18.8 miles on SR 353 to the village of Big Sandy (also unsigned in 1989). At an unmarked Y in the village go left 9 miles, crossing Big Sandy River, and then left again a final 11 miles to Big Sandy Campground. Pass the horse corral on the left, and in a few feet reach the road-end and Big Sandy trail No. 099 at the edge of the Bridger Wilderness, elevation 9150 feet.

Both the day hike and backpack follow the same trail along the cold Big Sandy River on a gentle rise in forest with a sprinkling of meadows. In $^1/_2$ mile is a junction with a choice. The Big Sandy trail and most of the horses go right, more or less following close to the water. An alternate trail No. 100 goes left, passing wooded Meeks Lake and at 2 miles V Lake before rejoining the Big Sandy trail, adding about $^1/_2$ mile to the trip and 200 feet of elevation gain. Meadows become more frequent and larger and finally dominate the scenery at the shores of $^1/_2$-mile-long Big Sandy Lake, 6 miles from the road-end, elevation 9690 feet, a rewarding turnaround point for a day hike— though the day-hiker is sure to be frustrated at lacking time to walk farther.

Before going on, take time here for two sidetrips—a short $1^1/_2$ miles through alpine meadows to Black Joe Lake, 10,258 feet, and a 2-mile trail to Clear and Deep Lakes, also ringed by meadows. Hike to the far end of Big Sandy Lake and find a junction. The left fork, trail No. 099, goes to Lonesome Lake; for the sidetrips go right on trail No. 116. In a few feet more come to a second junction. The left trail goes to Black Joe Lake; the right, trail No. 098, goes to Clear and Deep Lakes.

For Lonesome Lake—back at the Big Sandy Lake junction go left and follow North Creek through meadows 2 miles to a crossing of the Continental Divide at 10,600-foot Arrowhead Pass. Enter the Popo Agie Wilderness and drop to the shores of Lonesome Lake, 10,187 feet, $8^1/_2$ miles from the road.

The lake and surrounding meadows are impressive but the eyes are drawn to the Cirque of Towers, a ring of ten peaks all over 12,000 feet. From left to right: War Bonnet Peak, Warrior Peaks, Pylon Peak, Watch Tower, Block Tower, Sharks Nose, Overhanging Tower, Wolf Head, Camel's Hump, and Lizard Head Peak.

For more wandering or private camps, the trail continues, descending to North Popo Agie River valley.

Clark's nutcracker after summer snowstorm

2 ▪ Green River Lakes–Island Lake

DAY HIKE	BACKPACK
Green River Lakes	**Island Lake**
Round trip • 8 miles	Round trip • 52 miles
Hiking time • 4 hours	Hiking time • 5 days
High point • 8200 feet	High point • 10,799 feet
Elevation gain • 400 feet	Elevation gain • 2800 feet in, 1200 feet out

RESOURCES

Hikable • July through September
Management • Bridger–Teton National Forest
USGS maps • Green River Lakes, Square Top Mtn., Gannett Peak
Hiker map • Hiking Map & Guide, Northern Wind River Range, Earthwalk Press
Information • Pinedale Ranger District, P.O. Box 220, Pinedale, Wyoming 82941; phone (307) 367-4326
Permits • Not needed, but camping restrictions are in force; check with the Pinedale Ranger Station for specifics
Protection status • Bridger and Fitzpatrick Wildernesses

The Bridger Wilderness has over 500 miles of trail, 1300 lakes and ponds, and that many spectacular alpine vistas. Dozens of great hikes can be done there and in the adjoining Fitzpatrick Wilderness, to the hundred lakes accessible by trail—and the hundreds of others off the trails, which may or may not have fish but, if not, surely solitude. The great hike described here was selected because in addition to a goodly share of lakes it has a beautiful valley approach and gives opportunity for a loop. The dayhike sampler never reaches alpine vistas, but the two Green River Lakes, flowers, river, and forest are rewards enough.

Drive US 191 west of Pinedale 5.4 miles to between mileposts 105 and 106. Turn north on SR 352, signed "Cora and Green Rivers." At 25 miles enter national forest;

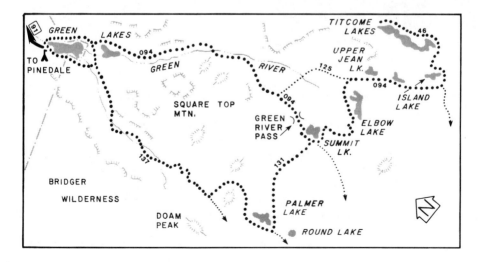

Green River, Square Top Mountain in distance

the road instantly deteriorates. At 45 miles the road ends at the first of the two Green River Lakes. The hikers' parking area and the beginning of Highline trail No. 094 are just outside the entrance to the campground, elevation 7961 feet.

A trail circles the first of the two Green River Lakes. On a hot afternoon, take the shady right-hand side of the lake; find that trail at the farthest end of the campground. Otherwise descend to the outlet, cross the Green River on a bridge, and walk the easier left-side trail. At 3 miles the two join. At 4 miles reach the second of the Green River Lakes, dominated by the odd-shaped mountain with a flat top, 11,695 feet high and named (surprise!) Squaretop Mountain. This is the turnaround point for the day hike.

The trail population thins as the backpacker continues past the lakes. The way alternates between forests and occasional meadows, following Green River upstream to the broad meadows of Three Forks Park and a footbridge across the river. From here the trail climbs over 10,370-foot Green River Pass and descends 100 feet to Summit Lake, 16 miles from the road, and a junction with a possible loop trip.

Excellent, very excellent. Is Summit Lake far enough? In these glacier-graded rock gardens are numerous lakes, puddles, and marshes. It's the kind of country that lures one on and on to see what the next lake looks like, what new sights will appear around the next bend, over the next rise. The map suggests a wealth of intriguing sidetrips, cross-country routes, and loops. Carry plenty of extra food—you'll want to stay two weeks, or until you're starving to death. For solitude, take map and compass in hand and get away from the trails.

For Island Lake, round Summit Lake staying on trail No. 094, keeping left (straight ahead) at the Doubletop Mountain trail No. 131 junction (the return section of the loop) and Pine Creek Canyon trail No. 165 junction, climbing past Elbow Lake at 10,777 feet. Go right at the Shannon Pass trail No. 125 junction to Upper Jean Lake at 10,799 feet, the highest point of the route. At Lower Jean Lake, 10,600 feet, go another 4 miles to a junction, then left 1 mile on trail No. 046, still in meadows, to Island Lake at 10,650 feet, 26 miles from the road. Spend another day exploring Lt. Fremont's 1842 route to the top of 13,745-foot Fremont Peak and look for the peak shown on the 1898 postage stamp entitled "Fremont on the Rocky Mountains."

For the loop mentioned before, return to Summit Lake and go left on the Doubletop Mountain trail No. 131 passing No Name, Cutthroat, and Palmer Lakes, down Palmer Canyon, up Dodge Creek, over 10,700-foot Porcupine Pass, and down Porcupine Creek to the starting point at lower Green River Lakes.

3 ▪ Granite Creek–Turquoise Lake

DAY HIKE
Granite Creek
Round trip • 8 miles
Hiking time • 3 hours
High point • 7400 feet
Elevation gain • 500 feet

BACKPACK
Granite Creek–Turquoise Lake
Round trip • 24 miles (28 miles from "official" trailhead)
Hiking time • 2 days
High point • 9460 feet
Elevation gain • 2500 feet

RESOURCES
Hikable • mid-June to mid-October
Management • Bridger–Teton National Forest
USGS maps • Granite Falls, Crystal Peak
Hiker map • Bridger–Teton National Forest Recreation Map
Information • Jackson Ranger Station, P.O. Box 1689, Jackson, Wyoming 83001; phone (307) 733-4755
Protection status • Gros Ventre Wilderness

People come to Jackson Hole by car, bus, and plane from all over America, Europe, Africa, and Asia, crowding the parking lots and spilling onto trails to see the world-famous view of the Teton Mountains rising like a picket fence above Jackson Hole.

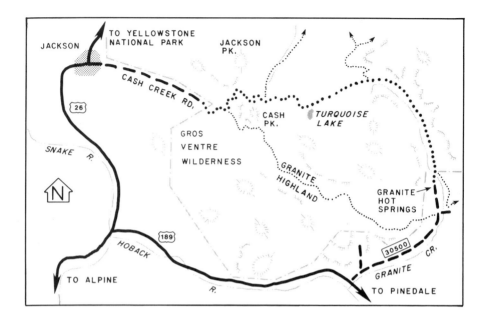

Few ever give a second glance east to the ordinary-looking rolling hills of the Gros Ventre (pronounced "grow vaunt") and few know about the trails that traverse ridge after ridge, inviting roaming mile after mile of alpine meadows interspersed with groves of slender evergreen trees and of aspen, whose leaves quake in the breeze and turn butter-yellow in fall. And there is wildlife—deer, elk, and moose, all out in the open in early morning. Trees, flowers, rivers, animals, and considerable solitude—that's surely enough to rate as great.

A short trail to Turquoise Lake starts right in the town of Jackson, so the lake is busy, but the other trails are not crowded. A person can stop to sniff the flowers or tie a shoelace without being run over by hordes of hikers, as happens, on the far side of Jackson Hole. This is horse country and the two fords of Granite Creek are easy for riders but guaranteed to cool a hiker's feet (and knees?).

A serious problem exists: For the benefit of the Granite Creek Hot Springs concessionaire, the hikers' trailhead has a sturdy locked gate completely blocking the trail. From 8 P.M. to 10 A.M. there is absolutely no way to get around or over the gate. Since hikers should be on the trail by 6 A.M. to see wildlife, they do best to start the evening before and camp a mile or two up the trail. Note that in an emergency it is impossible between 8 P.M. and 10 A.M. to return to the car to drive for help. When the gate was installed, horse people demanded and got a new trailhead that provided a bypass. Horses don't mind the extra 1½ miles each way, but few hikers want to walk the extra distance. If being trapped is a concern, it's best to park at the trailhead installed for horses, located downvalley near the Girl Scout camp, and start from there, adding an extra 3 miles round trip.

For the Granite Creek trail described here, drive highway 187/189 either north from Jackson or south from Pinedale to milepost 152 and turn onto the Granite Creek road, signed "Granite Creek Recreation Area," 8.7 miles to a junction just past Granite

Moose grazing along Granite Creek trail

Creek Campground. The right fork crosses Granite Creek to the lower (horse) trailhead; hikers go straight ahead another 1.6 miles to the hikers' trailhead and the parking area for the Granite Creek Hot Springs pool, elevation 6977 feet. Parking is reserved for the people using the pool; hikers must park alongside the road.

The trail crosses the gated Granite Creek bridge to the hot springs' pool where it joins the horse trail and heads upstream in a deep valley of alternating meadows and forest, always in sound of Granite Creek and the shadow of high cliffs. At 4 miles is the first ford, a good turnaround for day-hikers; the flowers, the river, and most likely the animals have by this point given a fair sampling of why the Gros Ventre trails are great.

The valley flattens and meadows begin. At 6½ miles, 8300 feet, is an intersection; a possible sidetrip climbs to 10,800 feet on the very crest of the Gros Ventre Range and meadows that lead toward the summit of 11,107-foot Pyramid Peak. For the lake continue on. The Granite Creek Trail passes marshes and finally climbs to Turquoise Lake, 9460 feet, 12 miles from the road-end.

Though not hiked by the authors, a return can be made by way of the Flat Creek–Crystal Creek loop or the Granite Highline trail, adding several extra days and more miles of meadows to the round trip.

4 • Lake Solitude

DAY HIKE	BACKPACK
Lake Solitude	**Lake Solitude Loop**
Round trip • 15 miles	Loop trip • 19 miles
Hiking time • 9 hours	Hiking time • 2 days
High point • 9024 feet	High point • 10,500 feet
Elevation gain • 2300 feet	Elevation gain • 3700 feet
Hikable • July to mid-October	Hikable • mid-July to October

RESOURCES

Management • Grand Teton National Park
USGS maps • Mt. Moran, Jenny Lake
Hiker map • USGS Grand Teton National Park
Information • Grand Teton National Park, Moose, Wyoming 83012; phone (307) 733-2880
Permits • Park Service camping permit required for overnight trips
Protection status • Grand Teton National Park

Lake Solitude is the destination of so many hikers and so many horses herded by commercial outfitters that solitude absolutely never is to be found, except maybe during a winter storm. But if the crowds destroy the wilderness mood, they can't mar the natural beauty of the lake, the wildflowers, and the pyramid summit of the Grand Teton looming above, three components of a great hike.

This hike can be done as a strenuous hike or a rather easy two-day loop. In both cases, Lake Solitude is the destination. Before planning a backpack, check with the rangers. Campsites are few, permits are required, and they are given only 1 day ahead, and in person. Get to the ranger station early; the limit at Lake Solitude is nine parties or 35 people. If you can't get space there, try for Paintbrush Canyon.

For the day hike drive to the large (huge) Jenny Lake parking area, 6700 feet. Early-morning hikers must hike around the south side of the lake, adding 2 miles. Late arrivals

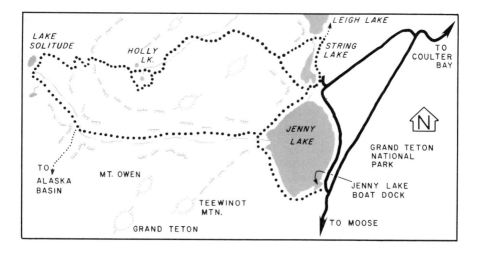

Glacier lilies beside Lake Solitude trail, Grand Teton in center

can save time by riding the tourist launch across the lake. Departure time and cost are posted at the nearby ticket booth. Backpackers should continue past Jenny Lake to the String Lake parking area, elevation 6700 feet, hike the String Lake trail a short distance, and go left on the Jenny Lake shore trail 2 miles to Hidden Falls. From there both day-hikers and backpackers follow the Cascade Canyon trail.

The Cascade Canyon trail switchbacks steeply over Hidden Falls into the canyon, a cleft between the rock walls of Storm Point and the icy cliffs of Mt. Owen and Teewinot Mountain. At 4¹/₂ miles, 7844 feet, go right. Forest thins to flower gardens. Look back to the top of Grand Teton rising above foreground summits. At 7¹/₂ miles is Lake Solitude, 9024 feet. Walk to the far end of the lake for the best views. Far enough for a day hike.

For the backpacker, to continue the loop, circle the south shore and climb through flowers and ever-expanding views to 10,500-foot Paintbrush Divide. From here the trail circles high above Holly Lake and descends a series of switchbacks to Paintbrush Canyon. The glacier-carved stair-step benches are famous for flowers. Look for the blue columbine and gentian and the red paintbrush for which the canyon was named. In the last 3 miles, the way leaves flowers for forest of spruce, fir, and lodgepole pine and returns to the starting point at String Lake.

5 • Shoshone Geyser Basin and Lake

DAY HIKE OR BACKPACK

Shoshone Geyser Basin and Lake

Round trip • 16 miles
Hiking time • 8 hours
High point • 8400 feet
Elevation gain • 800 feet in, 400 feet out

RESOURCES

Hikable • July to mid-October
Management • Yellowstone National Park
USGS maps • Craig Pass, Old Faithful, Shoshone Geyser Basin, Lewis Falls
Hiker map • Yellowstone National Park Trails Illustrated
Information • Yellowstone Library and Museum Association, Yellowstone National
    Park, Wyoming 80225; phone (307) 344-7381
Permits • Camping permits and reservations are required
Protection status • Yellowstone National Park

Hundreds of miles of trails in Yellowstone National Park are so lonesome a hiker can go days never seeing another person. This backcountry solitude is not famous. The thermal areas are. Still, there is a great hike that combines the hot-water show with more privacy than the Old Faithful area; though the Shoshone Geyser Basin is popular with horse-riders and canoeists as well as hikers, it is not totally overwhelmed by humanity. The geysers are not Old Faithfullike predictable; however, when they do go off it's with a gusto the more hair-raising for the surprise.

Reservations must be made in person, not more than 48 hours in advance. The notorious Yellowstone bears can be a factor in how many permits are given. Even in the absence of bears, only nine hiker campsites are available—lots of luck. If the luck is bad, the round trip can be done in a strenuous day.

The basin can be reached by canoe from Lewis Lake. Other trails lead in from Delacy Creek or, as described here, the Lone Star Geyser trailhead. Either start at Old Faithful

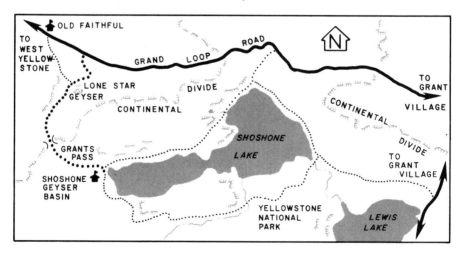

Union Geyser

or drive east 2.5 miles to the Lone Star Geyser trailhead, elevation 7583 feet.

The way follows the Firehole River on a gated service road. In 2¹/₂ miles pass Lone Star Geyser and the longer trail from Old Faithful. Go left on the Howard Eaton Trail 5¹/₂ miles through lodgepole pine forest, climbing gently over 8400-foot Grants Pass, and descend to the geyser basin on the shore of Shoshone Lake, 7791 feet.

Make camp and explore the geysers; Union Geyser is the largest, but it is unpredictable. However, perpetual steam vents and boiling hot springs are plentiful. Take care to stay on well-defined or boardwalk trails—in places a thin, solid-looking crust covers boiling water.

6 • Two Ocean Pass

DAY HIKE
None

BACKPACK
Two Ocean Pass
Loop trip • 52 miles
Hiking time • 5 days
High point • 10,315 feet
Elevation gain • 4200 feet

RESOURCES

Hikable • late June to November
Management • Bridger–Teton National Forest
USGS maps • Joy Peak, Two Ocean Pass, Mt. Hancock; for loop add Crater Lake, Ferry Lake, Joe Peak
Hiker map • Bridger–Teton National Forest Recreation Map
Information • Buffalo Ranger District, P.O. Box 278, Moran, Wyoming 83013; phone (307) 543-2386
Protection status • Teton Wilderness

No spectacular mountains, no glaciers, no alpine lakes, just miles and miles of rolling ridges, virgin forest, large meadows, and generally lots of solitude—all of which

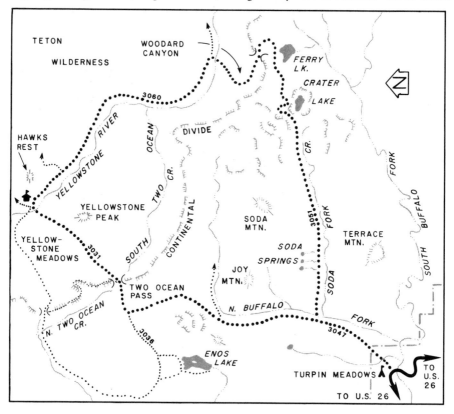

North Buffalo Fork

combine to abundantly earn the designation as a great hike. The trip does offer a unique if not very photogenic phenomenon, a creek that flows two different ways—to the Pacific Ocean and the Atlantic. A look at a map suggests a number of loops. Some are so long and remote one could travel a week or more, so far from civilization, singing, as in *They Call the Wind Mariah:* "... now I am lost, so dog-gone lost, that even God can't find me." The trail described here is neither the longest nor the shortest but includes the meandering headwaters of the Yellowstone River.

Be warned that this is horse country. At the trailhead we saw one (1) hikers' car and 26 horse trailers; nearby we noted several dude ranches. It is, therefore, a dusty

Aspen grove

(or muddy) and often stinking trail. However, this also is a big country, so big that a hiker may very well never meet another soul, afoot or ahorse.

From Jackson or the south entrance of Yellowstone National Park, drive to Moran Junction, then east on US 26/287 3.3 miles, and turn left on Buffalo River road 10 miles to Turpin Meadows and the North Buffalo Fork River trail, elevation 6916 feet.

The path enters forest, in ¹/₂ mile crosses Clear Creek, and at about 2 miles reaches the wilderness. The way goes up and down a bit skirting Soda Fork Meadows. At 5 miles is the junction with the Soda Fork trail, the return leg of the recommended loop. Follow North Buffalo Fork River past 3-mile-long North Fork Meadow. In another 5 miles leave the river, climb 600 feet, and enter Pacific Creek watershed and join the Atlantic–Pacific Trail at the west end of Two Ocean Pass, 8127 feet, 17 miles from the road.

Two Ocean Pass is a 2-mile-long marsh atop the Continental Divide, fed by both North Two Ocean Creek and South Two Ocean Creek. The marsh is the headwaters of both Pacific Creek and Atlantic Creek. Pacific Creek empties to the Snake River and eventually reaches the Pacific Ocean, while Atlantic Creek flows to the Yellowstone River and finally into the Gulf of Mexico. Momentous enough to earn the title "Parting of the Waters National Landmark."

For a sidetrip to tundra meadows with arctic-type flowers, hike the North Two Ocean Creek trail northward some 4 miles to rolling hills at 10,000 feet.

The pass is the beginning of a number of possible loops—all long, generally very lonesome, and most with river crossings that before midsummer are difficult to dangerous. One starts on the North Two Ocean Creek trail tracing the Continental Divide northward and returning via Mink Creek and Enos Lake. A longer loop goes over the Continental Divide at Phelps Pass and descends Mink Creek.

For the recommended loop described here, cross Two Ocean Pass and follow the Atlantic–Pacific Trail eastward down Atlantic Creek 4 miles to a ford of the Yellowstone River near Bridger Lake. Go upriver 13 miles, turning right 4¹/₂ miles up Woodard Canyon and a 10,313-foot crossing of the Continental Divide. Descend Soda Fork Creek trail 7 miles in a wide expanse of meadowland, passing Ferry Lake and 9330-foot Crater Lake, joining the North Buffalo Fork trail at the junction of the Buffalo River trail. To complete the loop, hike 5 miles back to the starting point at Turpin Meadows.

7 ▪ Mistymoon Lake–Solitude Trail Loop

DAY HIKE	BACKPACK
Mistymoon Lake	**Solitude Trail**
Round trip • 13 miles	Loop trip • 60 miles
Hiking time • 6 hours	Hiking time • 8 days
High point • 10,236 feet	High point • 11,000 feet
Elevation gain • 1136 feet	Elevation gain • 6600 feet

RESOURCES

Hikable • July to October

Management • Bighorn National Forest

USGS maps • Lake Angeline, Lake Solitude; for loop add Cloud Peak, Willow Pass, Shell Lake

Hiker map • Bighorn National Forest Recreation Map

Information • Bighorn National Forest, Buffalo Ranger District, 300 Spruce Street, Buffalo, Wyoming 82834; phone (307) 684-7981

Protection status • Cloud Peak Wilderness

Mistymoon Lake—what a name! And what a setting—glacier-chiseled granite cliffs, ice-gouged granite bowls brimming with icy water, and tundra vegetation reminiscent of the Arctic—three qualifications for greatness right there. But that's just a start: There are more lakes, granite bowls, and meadows. The wilderness is relatively small (most lakes can be reached by an easy day hike) but large enough for a magnificent week-

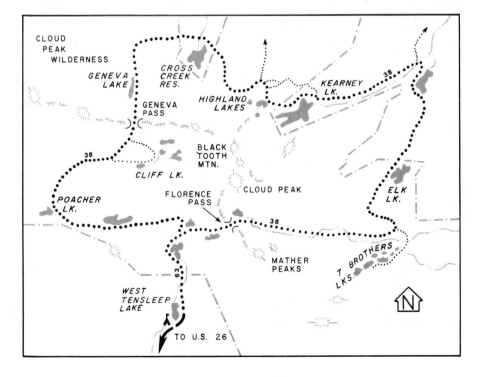

Mistymoon Lake

long backpack. Eastern license plates dominate the parking lots because this is the West's farthest-east wildland hiking area. A great many visitors feel the natural beauty isn't enough: They must also have fish. Therefore, stop by the lakes. Look your fill. Then go elsewhere to find private camping. Open ridges invite off-trail roaming.

Drive US 16 between Worland and Buffalo. At milepost 44, near Deer Haven Lodge, turn north 7 miles on West Tensleep Creek road No. 27 to West Tensleep Lake, elevation 9100.

The trail heads north, skirting the east side of the lake, crosses West Tensleep Creek on a sturdy bridge, and at 1 mile enters Cloud Peak Wilderness. Follow West Tensleep Creek through forest groves, small meadows, and marshes 4 miles to Lake Helen, 9968 feet, and the beginning of wide-open meadowland. At 6½ miles reach the clear blue waters of Mistymoon Lake, 10,236 feet. Note the fragile soil and the miniaturized plants, the mosslike mats of phlox and moss campion. The lake is an excellent day-hike turnaround, a superb sampling of the wilderness.

For the loop, go east 2 miles on Solitude Trail No. 38, over 11,000-foot Florence Pass to Florence Lake, 10,900 feet, and then 6 miles down Florence Canyon, beside North Clear Creek, into forest. The Solitude Trail goes left (north) at a junction—but first go right and make the easy 2-mile (each way) sidetrip to Seven Brothers Lakes, 9600 feet. To see all seven lakes, climb a hill. This is the most densely inhabited part of the wilderness. Don't camp here!

To continue the loop, at the junction enter forest and go north 9 miles past Elk Lake, 8863 feet, to Willow Creek Reservoir, 8616 feet. Turn left along the west side of the reservoir and in a scant mile go left again, up Kearney Creek to Kearney Lake, and climb to meadows of Highland Park, 10,900 feet. The trail drops into forest of the East Fork Big Goose valley and ascends to 10,300-foot Geneva Pass. Descend North Point Creek valley to Teepee Pole Flat, 9100 feet, and climb again to Lake Solitude and back to Mistymoon Lake.

MONTANA

Few experiences of the American earth are as thrilling as traveling westward in Big Sky country of the Great Plains, horizons infinite in all directions, and suddenly realizing the line of white clouds looming ahead is the snowcapped Rocky Mountains. The entirety of western Montana is occupied by various ranges of the Rockies, which extend south into Wyoming, west into Idaho, and north into Canada.

The mountains are mainly for hikers, with thousands of miles of delightful trails at elevations from 3000 to 11,000 feet. In the more easterly ranges, forests begin to thin at about 8000 feet and few trees grow above 10,000; the corresponding elevations are roughly 1500–2500 feet lower in the western part of the state. Some 106 small glaciers totaling 10 square miles are scattered in half a dozen ranges. One of the handful of summits that cannot be attained by walking or scrambling is 12,799-foot Granite Peak, Montana's highest, located in the Absaroka–Beartooth Wilderness. However, rockclimbers find numerous ice-plucked east and north faces of every degree of difficulty, the rock varying from solid granite to sedimentary and volcanic crud. The weather through June is often very wet and cold and the higher trails snowbound; July and August and the first half of September are generally fair except for afternoon thunderstorms.

Until the past generation, Montana was one great wildland, disrupted only here and there by residents, who with certain notorious exceptions blended almost Indianlike into the landscape. In the 1930s the immortal Bob Marshall and a few compatriots

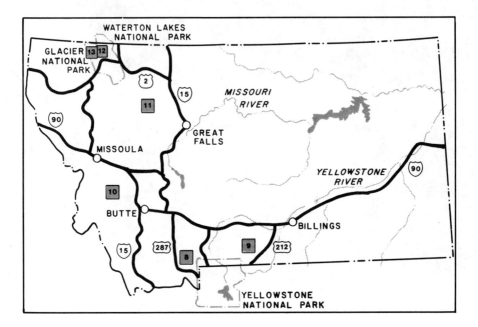

Ranger leading hikers on Grinnell Glacier

led the way toward gaining official dedication of some portions as wilderness, but there really seemed little danger that much of the backcountry would ever be radically altered. Now, however, the citizens of Montana are confronted by a proliferation of roads, off-road vehicles, and developers appropriating large areas for super-resorts. To protect the remaining trails, hikers and conservationists have worked to obtain a number of dedicated wildernesses, such as the Mission Mountains Wilderness, but there are many like the Ten Lakes Scenic Area that need protection; the task is far from complete.

The Lee Metcalf Wilderness is small but far enough from civilization that few people find it. The trail to Hilgard Lakes Basin (Hike 8) travels from forest to meadows to a basin of five lakes.

The Absaroka–Beartooth Wilderness offers hundreds of high mountain lakes and tundra meadows. It is a friendly wilderness that can, with a wisp of a cloud, turn very unfriendly; a balmy August morning can be succeeded by an afternoon blizzard. The Rainbow–Fossil Lakes trail (Hike 9) traverses a deep canyon to some of the most spectacular lakes.

In the Anaconda–Pintlar Wilderness, forest, steep alpine passes, rugged peaks, and lakes highlight Hike 10, while some of the lakes are easy day trips. The 35-mile Anaconda–Pintlar Loop reaches more.

Miles and miles of river-bottom trails are found in the Bob Marshall Wilderness. Hike 11, to the Chinese Wall, combines the forest valleys with a meadowland traverse under the Chinese Wall, where tectonic plates thrust up a 12-mile-long rock rampart.

Named for the Ice Age glaciers that shaped the park and their small successors, Glacier National Park has miles of trail. Grinnell Glacier (Hike 12) is a textbook display of glacier-carving, and the trail ends at a real, live (if tiny) glacier. The Garden Wall–Glenns Lake Loop (Hike 13) traverses miles of meadowland—excellent for a day or enough for a week.

Beargrass

8 • Hilgard Lakes Basin

DAY HIKE
Hilgard Pass
Round trip • 14 miles
Hiking time • 8 hours
High point • 9800 feet
Elevation gain • 3000 feet in, 200 feet
out

BACKPACK
Hilgard Lakes Basin
Round trip • 20 miles
Hiking time • 2 days
High point • 9800 feet
Elevation gain • 3000 feet in, 400 feet
out

RESOURCES

Hikable • late June through September
Management • Gallatin National Forest
USGS maps • Hilgard Peak, Pika Point
Hiker map • Gallatin National Forest (west half)
Information • Hebgen Lake Ranger District, West Yellowstone, Montana 59753;
   phone (406) 646-7369
Protection status • Lee Metcalf Wilderness

A delightful meadow basin, 3 square miles in area, contains five neatly hidden lakes—be sure to take USGS maps to find them. What with these Hilgard Lakes and the 11,000-foot peaks of the Madison Range, the trip meets most of the six conditions for a great hike, though the virgin forests are on the skimpy side and for perfect solitude in a fishing season a person may need to shun the lakes. Though steep in places and frustrating for its elevation losses, and sometimes badly chopped up by horses, the trail is fun. Starting in forest, within a mile small glades open up to large green meadows and finally alpine meadows. Yellow columbine blooms; higher, the yellow glacier lilies follow the snowline up the slopes.

From West Yellowstone drive north 8 miles on US 191 and 287. Go left on 287, passing Hebgen Lake (reservoir) at 15 miles, and then right on Beaver Creek road 4.4 miles to the road-end and trailhead parking lot, elevation 7200 feet.

Three trails leave the parking lot. For both the day hike and backpack take Sentinel

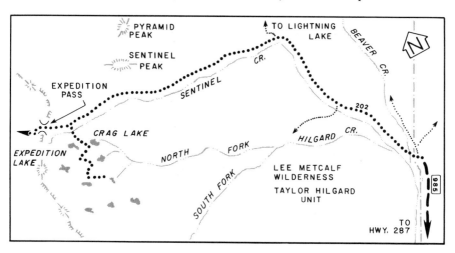

Crag Lake

Creek trail No. 202, signed "Expedition Pass 7 miles." The way drops to a crossing of Beaver Creek and begins a long ascent of the valley. At roughly 3 miles the seldom-used, unsigned Lightning Lake trail goes right. At 6^1/$_2$ miles the trail divides; leave the Expedition Pass trail and go left, crossing what remains of Sentinel Creek on boulders and climbing a final ^{1}/$_2$ mile to Hilgard Pass, 9800 feet, overlooking Hilgard Basin. Climb the knoll to the right for orientation; visible below are several lakes and a pond, dominated by 11,214-foot Echo Peak. The two large lakes below are Expedition and Crag Lakes. Get out the USGS map and figure out where the others are. This is the turnaround point for the day-hiker.

For backpackers, follow the trail very steeply down 200 feet to Expedition Lake and a wandering mile to Hand Lake, 9540 feet. Make a basecamp and spend one or two days exploring, actually finding those other lakes.

Rimrock Lake

9 ▪ Beartooth High Lakes Country

DAY HIKE OR BACKPACK	BACKPACK
Rainbow Lake	**Fossil Lake**
Round trip • 14 miles	Round trip • 30 miles
Hiking time • 7 hours	Hiking time • 3–7 days
High point • 7670 feet	High point • 9980 feet
Elevation gain • 1450 feet	Elevation gain • 3772 feet
Hikable • July through August	Hikable • mid-July through August
USGS map • Alpine (trail not shown)	USGS maps • Alpine, Cooke City (trails not shown)

RESOURCES

Management • Gallatin and Custer National Forests

Hiker map • Absaroka–Beartooth Mountains, produced by Rocky Mountain Surveys, P.O. Box 21558, Billings, Montana 59104-1558

Information • Gallatin National Forest, Federal Building, Bozeman, Montana 59715; phone (406) 587-4511; and Custer National Forest, 2602 1st Avenue N., Billings, Montana 59103; phone (406) 245-6361

Protection status • Absaroka–Beartooth Wilderness

A quick glance at the map explains why the Absaroka–Beartooth Wilderness is so popular. High mountains (including 12,799-foot Granite Peak, Montana's highest), rolling terrain, and over 300 lakes, many at or above timberline, are only the beginning. What the map can't show are the beautiful vistas, flower-covered meadows, and secluded campsites. Counting the good chance for solitude, we count four of the six qualities of a great hike.

The high lakes are accessible via Cooke City but the most dramatic (unforgettably scenic) entrance is the East Rosebud Creek trail. The way winds from lake to lake, following a raging torrent of a creek ("creek"!—in most of America it would rate as a full-grown river) and passing through a defile whose glacier-polished cliffs rise 1000 feet and more straight up. Except for being narrower, the valley is a veritable Yosemite look-alike.

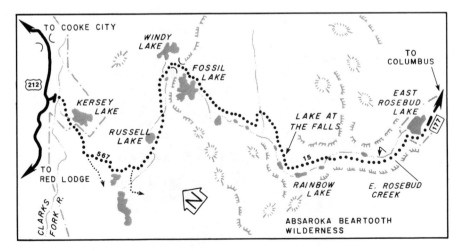

A pair of lovely subalpine lakes can be reached on a day hike and backpackers continue on to high alpine lakes, open tundra, and days of roaming.

Drive I-90 to Exit 408 (between Bozeman and Billings) and head through Columbus on SR 307. Take a right on SR 78. Pass the town of Absarokee at 15 miles from I-90 and at 28 miles go right on a road signed "Roscoe and East Rosebud Road." (This road can also be reached in 20 miles from Red Lodge.) Turn right at the junction, then left. In 4 miles cross East Fork Rosebud Creek and turn right on forest road No. 177 another 11 miles to East Rosebud Lake and 0.5 mile farther to the trailhead, elevation 6208 feet.

East Rosebud Creek trail No. 15 skirts private homes, in a long ¹/₂ mile enters the wilderness, and starts an easy climb to 6780-foot Elk Lake, about 3 miles (sign says 3¹/₂ miles), the destination of most day-hikers. Beyond the lake the way enters the narrow canyon of polished granite walls. At 4¹/₂ miles the path climbs a mile-long talus, the way sometimes blasted across the face of a cliff and sometimes skirting huge boulders. At 6 miles a bridge crosses the outlet of Rimrock Lake. At 7 miles reach a viewpoint above Rainbow Lake, 7670 feet, the turnaround for the day hike.

The trail skirts Rainbow Lake, and climbs to beautiful Lake at the Falls (a waterfall tumbles directly into the lake) at 9 miles, 8100 feet. Past Big Park Lake and Duggan Lake is Twin Outlets Lake, 9190 feet, 11 miles. Here begins the high alpine country, no fires allowed, the fragile vegetation crying out for low-impact camping. The route attains its 9980-foot high point at the west end of Fossil Lake, 15 miles from East Rosebud Lake, and the basecamp for days of exploring.

Experienced hikers will devise their own great treks by taking off cross-country to explore the numerous lakes not reached by formal trail. The high alpine terrain is relatively easy to travel but should not be done without a good map and compass; route finding is challenging in good weather and extremely difficult in poor. At these elevations snow may fall any day of summer; be properly garbed for a sudden spell of arctic conditions.

If transportation has been arranged for a one-way traverse, follow trail No. 15 another 9 miles, descending in forest to US 212 near Chief Joseph Campground, some 5 miles east of Cooke City.

Ptarmigan in summer plumage

10 ▪ Johnson Lake and the Anaconda–Pintlar Loop

DAY HIKE	BACKPACK
Johnson Lake	**Anaconda–Pintlar Loop**
Round trip • 9 miles	Loop trip • 35 miles
Hiking time • 5 hours	Hiking time • 4 days
High point • 7642 feet	High point • 9800 feet
Elevation gain • 1300 feet	Elevation gain • 6000 feet

RESOURCES

Hikable • mid-July to mid-October
Management • Deerlodge and Beaverhead National Forests
USGS maps • Warren Peak, Moose Lake; for loop add Kelly Lake, Carp Ridge
Hiker map • Anaconda–Pintlar Wilderness
Information • Philipsburg Ranger Station, P.O. Box H, Philipsburg, Montana 59762; phone (406) 859-3211
Protection status • Anaconda–Pintlar Wilderness

Johnson Lake, nestled under 9000-foot peaks, is a fine one-day sampler of the wilderness. The 35-mile loop, twice crossing the Continental Divide on 8000-foot passes, tours six lakes, miles of forest, and large expanses of mountain meadows. The abundance of fish rules out easy solitude and guns spook the wildlife, but four of the six criteria for a great hike are met. The Anaconda–Pintlar Wilderness is long and narrow, with access roads on all sides; the possibilities for day hikes therefore are numerous, including some of the lakes on the route of the loop. The lakes melt out in early July but the high passes are sometimes blocked with snow until August; call ahead to learn if they are passable for hikers.

Drive south of Drummond or west of Anaconda on SR 1 (shown on old maps as US 10A), and between mileposts 31 and 32 turn onto SR 38. At 9.3 miles from

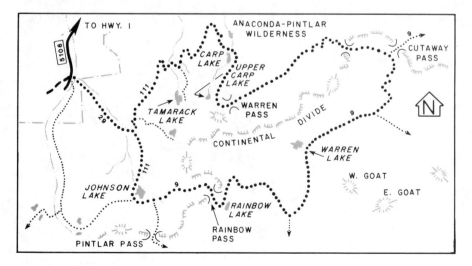

Huckleberries ready for picking

SR 1, go south on forest road No. 5106. Pass Moose Lake to the head of trail No. 29, elevation 6322, 15 miles from the highway.

The trail immediately enters Anaconda–Pintlar Wilderness and proceeds in forest along Falls Fork Rock Creek. At 2¹/₂ miles is a junction, 7200 feet, with trail No. 111; to the left is the return leg of the loop. Keep right (straight ahead) another 2 miles to Johnson Lake, 7642 feet, a satisfying day-hike turnaround.

For the loop, continue around the lake and stay left at the first junction, then left on trail No. 9 (don't confuse with trail No. 9 headed for Pintlar Pass), climbing a steep 2 miles over Rainbow Pass on the Continental Divide at 9040 feet. Drop equally steeply to Rainbow Lake, 8215 feet, 8 miles from the road-end.

Keep left at the lake on trail No. 9, descending in forest 3¹/₂ miles to 7400 feet. Go left 2 miles, still on trail No. 9, crossing an easy 8600-foot pass to 8462-foot Warren Lake, 14 miles from the road. From Warren, considered the most beautiful lake in the whole wilderness, descend 2 miles along West Fork LaMarche Creek to a junction at 7400 feet. Keep left, staying on trail No. 9, and climb 2¹/₂ miles to 9400-foot Cutaway Pass. At the junction here keep left on trail No. 111, contouring 1¹/₂ miles along the south side of the ridge to the second crossing of the Continental Divide at 9800 feet. The trail drops 2200 feet in 4 miles to a tributary of Carp Creek and climbs again to a small lake in Maloney Basin. Climb over 8600-foot Warren Pass to Upper Carp Lake, 8400 feet, 27 miles from the road.

From Upper Carpp Lake the trail descends to Carp Lake. Cross the inlet, climb a bit, and drop to Tamarack Creek. Again stay left on trail No. 111 to a junction with a recommended sidetrip of 1¹/₂ miles (3 miles round trip) to 8300-foot Tamarack Lake, dominated by 10,463-foot Warren Peak. In another 2¹/₂ miles is a short sidetrip that climbs 400 feet to Edith Lake, 7800 feet. In ¹/₂ mile complete the loop and rejoin the Johnson Lake trail at a point just 2¹/₂ miles from the road.

Johnson Lake after late-summer storm

11 · The Chinese Wall

DAY HIKE
None

BACKPACK
The Chinese Wall–Spotted Bear Pass
Round trip • 70 miles
Hiking time • 8 days
High point • 7200 feet
Elevation gain • 2200 feet

RESOURCES
Hikable • July through September
Management • Lewis and Clark National
  Forest
USGS maps • Scapegoat Mtn., Amphi-
  theater Mtn., Glenn Crew, Prairie
  Reef, Pretty Prairie
Hiker maps • Lewis and Clark National
  Forest Recreation Maps
Information • Rocky Mountain Ranger
  District, Box 340, Choteau, Mon-
  tana 59422; phone (406) 466-5341
Protection status • Bob Marshall Wil-
  derness

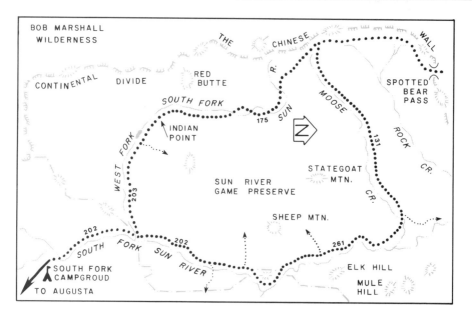

Aerial view of Chinese Wall

The Bob Marshall Wilderness, together with the Great Bear Wilderness, Scapegoat Wilderness, and Sun River Game Preserve, constitute the largest wilderness area in the contiguous 48 states. To be frank, it is the fame—of the spaciousness of the wildland and of the man whose name is memorialized—that gives the trip its chief claim to its status as great. However, there are large forests, many streams, a few flowers and views, and the grizzlies certainly qualify as wildlife. Solitude is possible with a bit of planning. Lakes are few and trails are long and heavily used by horses. The distances are so great that a week or more should be planned for any hike.

Despite the overwhelming number of horses, over half the users are afoot. The attraction is the opportunity to "get away from it all" for weeks at a time—escaping even the horses in the maze of peaceful sidetrails. There is no easy way to sample the heart of the wilderness, though the essence can be guessed on the 2-mile hike to the west side's Upper Holland Lake or a short wander up the South Fork Flathead River.

The suggested backpack is the most scenic destination in the whole wilderness. The name was borrowed from the 2000-mile Chinese Wall built to fend off roaming hordes of Mongolians. The American construction was accomplished by a titanic collision of tectonic plates deep in the earth that thrust up a wall of limestone, 200–800 feet high, which for 12 miles effectively forbids the hordes of hikers and horsemen from crossing the Continental Divide. The wall's west side is a gentle slope; it's the dramatic east side that does the stopping.

Be warned: Grizzly bears have the right-of-way, whether you grant it willingly or not. The troops of heavy cavalry take the right-of-way from both grizzlies and pedestrians, especially during the fall hunting season. The best bet for hikers is early summer.

From SR 287 on the south edge of the town of Augusta, drive west on forest road No. 434. At 0.2 mile turn right on Benchmark Road No. 235, at 25 miles pass Wood Lake, at 31.5 miles keep right toward the South Fork Campground, and at 32 miles reach the trailhead, elevation 5250 feet, the jump-off for a number of popular trails.

Follow South Fork Sun River trail No. 202 downstream. In ¼ mile cross a sturdy suspension bridge and proceed through lodgepole pine. At 4½ miles turn left on trail No. 203, following West Fork (of the) South Fork Sun River upstream, still in lodgepole forest. Pass several sidetrails and a number of campsites. At 11 miles from the road-end, the trail becomes No. 175. Campsites are fewer as the way climbs steadily to open meadows at the foot of the Chinese Wall and, at 7200 feet, the last possible camp with water, some 18 miles from the road.

The trail hugs the base of the Chinese Wall 8 miles (in season, wildflowers will be blooming), drops a bit to Spotted Bear Pass, 6271 feet, and an opportunity to look over to the west side of the Continental Divide.

For variety a slightly longer return can be made on Moose Creek trail No. 131, down to North Fork Sun River trail No. 261 and back up South Fork Sun River trail No. 202 to the road-end at Benchmark. If using this route, check first—in the high water of snowmelt season the ford may be unsafe or impossible for hikers.

Stonecrop

12 ▪ Grinnell Glacier

DAY HIKE
Grinnell Glacier
Round trip • 12 miles
Hiking time • 6 hours
High point • 6400 feet
Elevation gain • 1500 feet

BACKPACK
None

RESOURCES

Hikable • mid-July through September
Management • Glacier National Park
USGS map • Many Glaciers
Hiker map • USGS Glacier National Park
Information • Glacier National Park, West Glacier, Montana 59936; phone (406) 888-5441
Protection status • Glacier National Park

Every wildland walker wants sometime to set foot on a living glacier. The name of the National Park ("glacier! wow!") thus makes it the mecca of legions upon legions of feet from the Midwest and East, visitors unaware that the glaciers here are few and small compared to those in ranges farther west and close by to the north. But this by no means is to poormouth the Grinnell Glacier. It *is* a glacier, and for most who come here, the first glacier of their lives. Those from icier mountains may be somewhat amused by the presumption of the Grinnell, but they are definitely impressed by the trail, which offers a quintessential experience of Glacier National Park's array of peaks sculpted by ancient glaciers into blocky massifs standing awesomely tall and steep above the broad, deep troughs gouged by those old glaciers!

The park has some 800 miles of trails of all degrees of difficulty, none truly lonesome, none more popular than this easy walk. The serendipity of this great hike (the ideal newcomer's introduction to the park) is the ranger-naturalist who leads guided hikes

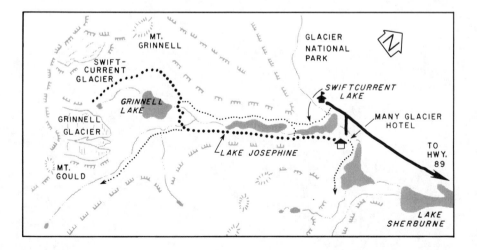

at a pace slow enough to suit the most sluggish feet, enriching the day with identification of plants and explanations of the geology and wildlife *(Ursus horribilis)*. Because few visitors from the East come equipped with ice axe and knowledge of snow travel, in early summer the Park Service "opens" the snow-covered trails with blasting wire and, until this is done, posts the trails "closed."

From US 89 on the east side of Glacier National Park, drive to Many Glacier Hotel on Swiftcurrent Lake and find the parking lot near the ranger station, elevation 4896 feet.

The trail circles Lake Josephine, so if making the trip on your own, start on either side of the lake or even ride the tourboat to the far end. Lake Josephine is a "long lake" filling a trough "over-deepened" by the scouring ice and passes near Grinnell Lake, a "round lake" set in a huge cirque plucked from dramatic cliffs. The contrast between calm blue waters and vaulting mountain walls is of the essence of the park; often an afternoon wind stirs those calm waters to a frenzy of whitecaps and loud waves thrashing the beaches.

The trail climbs in earnest from the cirque floor, the views growing down to the lakes and across to the massive solid geometry of the gigantic mountain blocks. At one point the way traverses a cliff of red rock on a ledge 4 feet wide—airy but not dangerous. At others, in early summer, it proceeds across snowfields on the trail blasted out by the rangers. At 6 miles, 6400 feet, the trail ends in a heap of moraine rubble beside little Upper Grinnell Lake and the little Grinnell Glacier, beneath the summit ridge of Mt. Gould.

Unless accompanied by a ranger-naturalist, don't set foot on the glacier. Be content with the close look at the living ice and precipices of the upper cirque—which happen to be the backside of the Garden Wall. Note windows in the cliff near the top. A drop of rain hitting this knife-thin ridge on the exact crest would be split in two, half flowing to the Atlantic Ocean and half to the Pacific.

Opposite: *Ranger-led group on Grinnell Glacier trail.* Above: *Ptarmigan walking on Grinnell Glacier trail*

13 ▪ The Garden Wall–Glenns Lake Loop

DAY HIKE, BACKPACK, OR
CHALET-HOP
The Garden Wall
Round trip • 15 miles
Hiking time • 7 hours
High point • 7200 feet
Elevation gain • 600 feet in, 700 feet
  out

BACKPACK
Glenns Lake Loop
Loop trip • 71 miles
Hiking time • 8 days
High point • 7600 feet
Elevation gain • 8300 feet

RESOURCES

Hikable • mid-July through September
Management • Glacier National Park
USGS maps • Logan Pass, Many Glaciers; for loop add Mt. Cannon, Ahern Pass,
  Mt. Cleveland, Porcupine Ridge
Hiker map • USGS Glacier National Park
Information • Glacier National Park, West Glacier, Montana 59936; phone (406)
  888-5441
Permits • Backcountry permit required for overnight use; space at chalets must be
  reserved—usually months ahead
Protection status • Glacier National Park

The highway over Logan Pass is on everybody's short list of North America's most
magnificent mountain drives. Without ever leaving the car, it's great. Well then, why
leave the car? The views are as spectacular from the road as from the trail, the fields
of alpine flowers as brilliant. Ah, but hikers smell the flowers rather than automobile

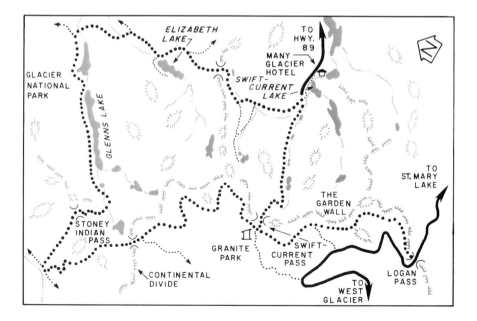

Heavens Peak and McDonald Creek valley

exhaust, and at 2 mph they can savor the views much more fully than at 45 mph on a narrow road, hasty drivers tailgating and enraptured drivers abruptly jamming on brakes to admire a deer. Furthermore, the hiker has a good chance to meet not only deer but bighorn sheep and, if lucky, mountain goats. (He may or may not feel lucky to meet a grizzly bear—when *Ursus* is known to be around, any park trail may be closed.)

Glacier, like other national parks, has very restrictive backcountry camping rules. If a backpacker doesn't care where he goes, chances are there will always be a place to camp. However, anyone planning an eight-day trip, such as described here, may have trouble getting the needed campsites during the first three weeks of August. Campsites can only be reserved in person and not more than 24 hours in advance. The best advice is to be at a visitors center by 8 A.M. and hope.

From West Glacier or St. Mary, drive the Going-to-the-Sun Highway to the large parking lot and visitors center at Logan Pass, elevation 6646 feet. On the north side of the road find the trailhead, signed "Granite Park Chalet."

Bighorn sheep along trail

The two trips we describe here are both great. The short one, the Garden Wall, is second in popularity only to Grinnell Glacier. Traversing a wide bench near the rocky crest of the Continental Divide, with the Grinnell Glacier on the other side of the ridge, the trail's mood on this side is not the cold white of ice but the warm rainbow of flowers. In relatively minor ups and downs the way leads northward through meadows beneath cliffs of the Garden Wall to Granite Park Chalet, 6500 feet, 7¹/₂ miles from Logan Pass. This is the turnaround point. If reservations have been made, a hiker can either camp, stay at the chalet, or retrace the route back to Logan Pass, a very long but rewarding day's effort.

At the chalet is a four-way junction; the left fork drops steeply to forest and highway; the right fork climbs over Swiftcurrent Pass to the Many Glaciers Hotel. The loop proceeds straight ahead, continuously spectacular, another 12¹/₂ miles along the crest of the Continental Divide before dropping in 5¹/₂ miles to 4400 feet in the Waterton River valley, 25 miles from Logan Pass. From the river the trail climbs 2¹/₂ miles to Stoney Indian Lake, 6325 feet, and 1 more switchbacking mile to Stoney Indian Pass, 6908 feet, 27¹/₂ miles from Logan Pass. A 4-mile descent ensues to 2¹/₂-mile-long Glenns Lake, and 5 more miles to a junction with the Ptarmigan Trail, 4800 feet, 39 miles from Logan Pass and the approximate halfway point of the loop.

Follow the Ptarmigan Trail a moderate 4 miles to Elizabeth Lake, the start of a 7-mile climb up the Ptarmigan Wall. At 7600 feet duck through a rock tunnel and descend 5 miles to a motel, hotel, and store at Swiftcurrent Lake, 4875 feet. The final leg is 8 miles over 7185-foot Swiftcurrent Pass to Granite Park Chalet and 7¹/₂ miles to the starting point at Logan Pass.

IDAHO

I daho north of the Snake River plains is one grand maze of mountains, sagebrush-covered on lower slopes, forested from 4000–6000 feet up to 9000–10,000 feet, above that sculptured by Pleistocene glaciers into cliffs and cirques now bare of ice but with summer snowfields and rocky parks and sparkling lakes and flowery meadows. Attractive as are the highlands, the canyons are perhaps even better known—certainly among river-runners.

Until recently the state's wilderness was so vast and empty it was a great place for a person to get so lost nobody could even begin a search. Then came jet-set dude ranches, an uncontrolled invasion by jeeps and the "poor man's horse" (the motorcycle), and simultaneous movement into the backcountry by loggers and dammers and big-corpo-

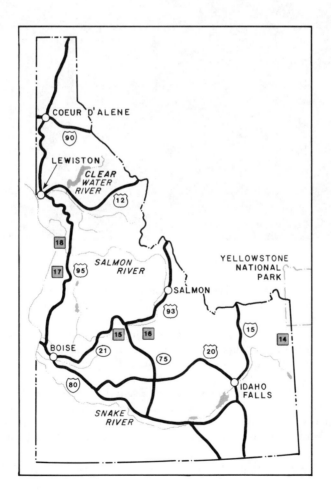

Teton Crest, Jedediah Smith Wilderness

ration miners. And lo! It was realized that Idaho is, after all, finite. As a result, some of the nation's hottest wildland battles were fought in the 1970s, and partly won, partly lost (but conservationists have regrouped to fight on).

Though some areas no longer are worth walking and others are now crowded, there still is plenty of room for a hiker to be lonesome and enchanted. Except for granite spires of the Sawtooths, few peaks challenge expert climbers, but the off-trail scrambler can find good fun everywhere.

The Jedediah Smith Wilderness is on the relatively unknown backside of Grand Teton National Park or, more precise, the west slopes of the Grand Teton Range. It lacks the famous views of the Grand (and the mobs), but it does have more alpine meadows and more miles of ridge-top trails. The essence is caught in Hike 14, the Devils Stairway–Fox Creek Pass trail.

Located only a hop, skip, and a short jump from Sun Valley, the lakes and flowers

and peaks of the Sawtooth Wilderness have earned well-deserved popularity among hikers. Short trails to alpine lakes are crowded with day-hikers but longer trails are relatively lonesome, including much of the wilderness traverse described in Hike 15.

One should spend weeks and months exploring the trails in the White Cloud Peaks Proposed Wilderness and on Mt. Borah in the Pioneer Mountains. Our pick is two seldom-visited lake basins, Boulder Chain Lakes Basin and Big Boulder Lakes Basin (Hike 16).

In the Hells Canyon National Recreation Area, the Snake River trail (Hike 17) winds 31 miles upstream in North America's deepest canyon, popular with river-rafters but little known by hikers.

The Seven Devils Range, located in the Hells Canyon Wilderness, is loaded with lakes, rugged peaks, and alpine meadows. Far from any metropolitan area and little known, solitude mixed with beauty can be found in Hike 18, the Seven Devils Loop.

14 • Table Mountain–Devils Stairway

DAY HIKE	BACKPACK
Table Mountain	**Devils Stairway–Fox Creek Pass**
Round trip • 13 miles	Round trip • 26 miles
Hiking time • 8 hours	Hiking time • 3 days
High point • 11,106 feet	High point • 9760 feet
Elevation gain • 4100 feet	Elevation gain • 2700 feet in, 300 feet out

RESOURCES

Hikable • mid-July through September
Management • Jedediah Smith Wilderness
USGS maps • Mt. Bannon, Grand Teton, Granite Basin, Mt. Moran, Remmel Mountain
Hiker map • Targhee National Forest Recreation Map
Information • Teton Basin Ranger District, Targhee National Forest, Driggs, Idaho 83422; phone (208) 354-2431
Protection status • Jedediah Smith Wilderness

Trails from Jackson Hole on the east side of Grand Teton National Park are generally crowded. To be more precise, mobbed. Trails from the west, or Idaho, side of the Tetons are less crowded, are merely very busy. Don't be put off by the population density—the wildflowers and scenery are some of the best of the Rocky Mountains, fully great and well worth the sociability.

For both the day hike and the backpack, drive SR 33 to Driggs, Idaho, and go east on Little Avenue, signed "Alta" and "Grand Targhee Recreational Area." At 6 miles

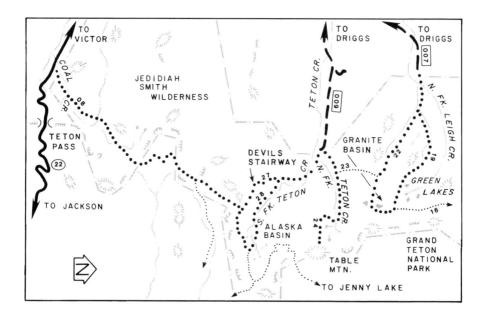

South Fork Teton Creek

leave the paved road and go right on forest road No. 09 another 5 miles to the Table Mountain trailhead, elevation 6900 feet, for the day hike and a bit farther to the road-end at the South Fork trailhead, elevation 6955 feet, for the longer hike.

Some 200 hikers a day strenuously ascend to Table Mountain's staggering views of Cascade Canyon and the Grand Teton. The day hike starts at the upper corner of the Table Mountain parking area on trail No. 024, enters Jedediah Smith Wilderness, and follows the North Fork Teton Creek. In a long mile keep straight ahead at a junction with the Leigh Creek trail No. 023; after 6 1/2 steep miles of forest and meadow gaining 4100 feet, reach the summit's cliff-edge 11,106-foot viewpoint.

The backpack starts on South Fork trail No. 027, immediately enters the Jedediah Smith Wilderness, and ascends the glacier trough of Teton Canyon. At 2 3/4 miles reach a junction and a decision. Both trails go to the same place. The trail straight ahead follows the delightful creek, emerging from forest to the meadows of Alaska Basin and a group of small lakes. The right fork is a mile longer and has a 1200-foot climb in 1 mile up Devils Stairway but gets to alpine country faster and—oh! the view! The logical plan is to go up one way and down the other.

For the Devils Stairway, go right, cross the creek, and ascend the switchbacks up the grueling western wall of Teton Canyon to a wide, sloping shelf between layers of the tilted sedimentary rock that overlie the granite heart of the Tetons. The trail traverses the flower-covered shelf in 3½ miles of ever-expanding views and then descends 200 feet to Alaska Basin and Sunset Lake, set in a small bowl scooped from the granite by glaciers.

Alaska Basin is good enough and far enough for most hikers. (Most hikers start at Jenny Lake, inside the national park, and ascend Cascade Canyon. That's why the Idaho approach, just as scenic, is less busy.) The full hike offers many more miles of high-level hiking. Pick up the Skyline Trail, cross 9760-foot Mt. Meek Pass 10 miles from the trailhead, enter Grand Teton National Park, and follow Death Canyon shelf another 3 scenic miles to Fox Creek Pass, 9600 feet. The Skyline Trail zigs in and out of the park another 15 miles to SR 22 near Teton Pass.

While discussing great hikes, not to be ignored is the full length of the Skyline Trail running near the crest of the Teton Range from Teton Pass north some 28 miles to Dry Ridge, with views down west to farms in Teton Basin (originally called Pierre's Hole, as Jackson Hole originally was called simply Big Hole), east to the aspects few folks see of the Grand, Mt. Owen, Mt. Moran, and a row of other spectacular peaks, the entire way in mile after mile of flowers, the bloom climaxing in late July and early August.

For the northern portion of the Skyline Trail, start on Table Mountain trail No. 024, in a mile go left on trail No. 023 to trail No. 021, and finally on Skyline Trail No. 008. Or, for a shorter route, drive north from Driggs on SR 33 for 5.4 miles. Just north of the South Fork Leigh Creek crossing, where the highway curves left, go right and right again on Leigh Creek road. At 3 miles from the highway, turn left on North Fork Leigh Creek road another 6.7 miles to the Green Mountain trailhead, elevation about 7000 feet, and then hike trail No. 019 to the Skyline Trail.

Steer's head (flower) beside Devils Stairway trail

15 • Sawtooth Lake–Sawtooth Wilderness Traverse

DAY HIKE
Sawtooth Lake
Round trip • 10 miles
Hiking time • 5 hours
High point • 8430 feet
Elevation gain • 1700 feet

BACKPACK
Sawtooth Wilderness Traverse
Round trip • 64 miles
Hiking time • 10 days
High point • 9500 feet
Elevation gain • 7699 feet in, 5900 feet out

RESOURCES

Hikable • mid-July to October
Management • Sawtooth National Recreation Area
USGS maps • Stanley Lake; for traverse add Warbonnet Peak, Mt. Cramer, Snowyside Peak, Mt. Everly
Hiker map • Hiking Map & Guide Sawtooth Wilderness (commercial)
Information • Stanley Ranger Station, Star Route HC64, P.O. Box 9900, Stanley, Idaho 83278; phone (208) 774-3681
Permits • Wilderness permit required for parties of more than eight
Protection status • Sawtooth Wilderness

The development-free Sawtooth Mountains lie a mere hop and a skip from the glitz of Sun Valley, and the drive-to lakes and easy day hikes are crowded with tourists wearing white shorts, white socks, and white shoes, as well as wilderness hikers in every manner and color of garb. Whatever their experience level and endurance, all come away well

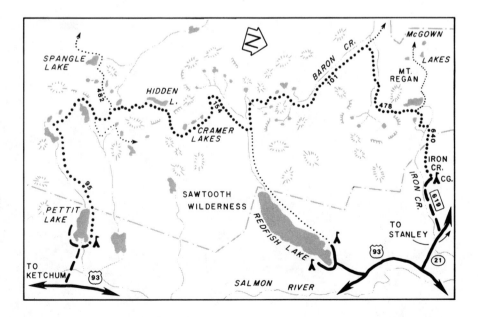

rewarded by mountain lakes, rugged peaks, and a generous supply of wildflowers. What more is required to be a great hike? Solitude! The backpacker can add that to the rewards, for once beyond day-hiker reach, the trails are next to empty and among the several dozen lakes at least one is likely to offer total privacy. (If making the traverse check ahead to be sure all stream crossings are in good shape.)

From the town of Stanley, drive west 2.5 miles on SR 21. Between mileposts 128 and 129, turn left 3.2 miles on Iron Creek road No. 619, signed "Iron Creek Campground," to the trailhead at Iron Creek Transfer Camp, elevation 6710 feet.

In 1 mile the forest trail enters Sawtooth Wilderness. In 1½ miles is a junction; go right ½ mile, then left. The way climbs past rugged cliffs, switchbacking to a welcome rest at Alpine Lake, 4 miles, 7823 feet, and then continues to Sawtooth Lake, 8430 feet, 5 miles from the road. This is a good day-hike turnaround and a sample of things to come. Overnighters with extra energy will find a smaller population if they turn right at the lake, climbing 400 feet and dropping 300 feet to the three McGown Lakes, 8505 feet.

For the wilderness traverse, at Sawtooth Lake go left, round the shore, and climb over an 8500-foot shoulder of Mt. Regan. Descend 7 miles into the forested North Fork Baron Creek valley and a junction at 5600 feet. Go left along Baron Creek, climbing 7 miles out of the valley to the three Baron Lakes, 8312 feet. The trail climbs another 1 mile over a 9100-foot ridge and 2 miles more past 8331-foot Alpine Lake (yes, this is the second Alpine Lake) to a junction with the Redfish Lake trail, 7400 feet. Go right 4 miles to the three Cramer Lakes, 8381 feet.

Again the trail crosses a high divide, 9500 feet, and in 2 miles passes Hidden Lake, 8200 feet. Many switchbacks lead to Edna Lake, 8404 feet, 32 miles from the Iron Creek road-end. Beyond are Ardith Lake, Spangle Lake, Lake Ingeborg, and lakes and more lakes, too many to list, and still more in the headwaters of the Payette and Boise Rivers. (It should be noted that these last lakes are accessible via a shorter trail from Pettit Lake Campground.)

Opposite: *Sawtooth Lake and Mount Regan*
Above: *Sawtooth Lake from McGowan Basin trail*

16 ▪ Boulder Chain Lakes–Big Boulder Lakes

DAY HIKE
None

BACKPACK
Boulder Chain Lakes–Big Boulder Lakes
Round trip • 48 miles
Hiking time • 5 days
High point • 9800 feet
Elevation gain • 3800 feet

RESOURCES

Hikable • mid-July to mid-October
Management • Sawtooth National Recreation Area
USGS maps • Boulder Chain Lakes, Bowery Creek
Hiker map • None, use Sawtooth National Forest Recreation Map
Information • Stanley Ranger Station, Star Route HC64, P.O. Box 9900, Stanley,
    Idaho 83278; phone (208) 774-3681
Protection status • Unprotected

Lakes galore: big cirque lakes, chain lakes, little tarns, ponds, marshes, bogs, and swamps. Plus beautiful meadows and forest and the White Cloud Peaks. That does for four of the six great criteria. Motorcycles on the main trails so discourage most hikers that the lakes basin, which otherwise would be a people-swarm, actually satisfy a fifth criteria—some *solitude!*

Two sets of lakes have direct trails. Both basins are beautiful but different enough that both demand visits, either on separate hikes, or by use of two cars, or tied together as a loop, or, as described here, a round trip.

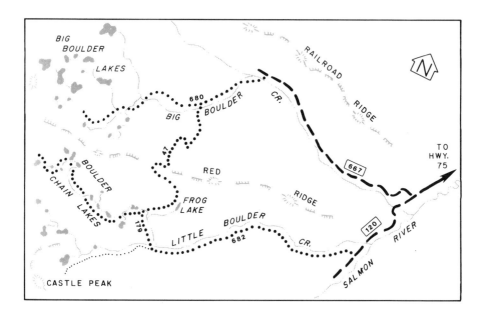

Castle Peak from Little Boulder Creek trail

For years environmentalists and hikers have been trying to ban motorcycles on these trails, but so far the off-road vehicle lobby has been more effective. At least the lake basins are motor-free.

From near milepost 227 on SR 75, turn south on the East Fork Salmon River road, signed "Dump Station." At 18 miles make a decision based on which is the stronger, you or your car. If the car, take the right fork up a steep and hairy 4.5-mile mining road to the Big Boulder Creek trailhead, elevation 7000 feet. The recommended approach combines a road that is easier on the car with a trail that takes more out of the hiker: Drive the left fork 2 comfortable miles to Little Boulder Creek trail No. 682, elevation 6100 feet.

The Little Boulder Creek trail climbs a sagebrush hillside, levels off, enters meadowland along the creek, and at about 7 miles comes to a junction with Castle Lake trail No. 047; go right, crossing the creek. In 1 more mile, 8 miles from the road, is another junction, 8800 feet. The right fork leads to Big Boulder Lakes. But for now go left on trail No. 683 into Boulder Chain Lakes Basin, leaving motorcycle problems behind, and in the next 5 miles pass Willow Lake, the four Chain Lakes, campsites at Hourglass Lake, and Boulder Lake, ending at Headwall Lake (a total of eight lakes), 13 miles from the road. Bootbeaten paths lead to eleven more off-trail lakes.

For Big Boulder Lakes Basin, retrace the trail 5 miles to Willow Lake and go left 6 miles on the motorcycle "trail" past Frog Lakes, across a 9500-foot divide, and descend to the Big Boulder Creek trail No. 680. Turn left, cross the creek on a log that stops all wheels, and enjoy the peace and quiet of a real trail. Hike upstream 5 miles to Walker, Hook, and Cove Lakes and four more reached on primitive paths in Big Boulder Basin, 9800 feet.

Either return the way you came or, if a car pickup is available there, return 6 miles along the Big Boulder Creek trail to Big Boulder road, 7300 feet.

17 • Hells Canyon–Snake River Trail

DAY HIKE	BACKPACK
Kirkwood Living Historic Ranch	**Snake River Trail**
Round trip • 10 miles	Round trip • 62 miles
Hiking time • 5 hours	Hiking time • 6–8 days
High point • 1600 feet	High point • 1600 feet
Elevation gain • 400 feet	Elevation gain • 1000 feet
Hikable • April to October	Hikable • April to May and September
USGS map • Kernan Point	to October
	USGS maps • Kernan Point, He Devil

RESOURCES

Management • Hells Canyon National Recreation Area
Hiker map • Hells Canyon National Recreation Area Map
Information • Hells Canyon National Recreation Area, 3620-B Snake River Road,
    Lewiston, Idaho 83501; phone (208) 743-3648
Protection status • Hells Canyon National Recreation Area

Hells Canyon is definitely not paradise. Summer temperatures soar above 100 degrees, rattlesnakes abound, poison ivy grows in profusion, and, despite the river, drinkable water can be hard to find. However, as one of the nation's most awesome chasms, naked slopes rising nearly a mile straight up from the Snake River to mountain crests, hiking there is an unforgettable experience. Both the Idaho and Oregon sides of the canyon have little-used river-level trails. Access is difficult on the Idaho side and worse on the Oregon side. The Idaho trail is open most of the year but sections of the Oregon route may be flooded during high water.

A day hike to Kirkwood Living Historic Ranch is a good sampling of the canyon, sufficient for most, giving excellent vantages of the uniquely beautiful scenery. Watching dories and rafts take the rapids and the tourist-loaded jet boats scream up and down the river provides constant entertainment.

The great hike, of course, is the 31-mile journey to Granite Creek. The canyon

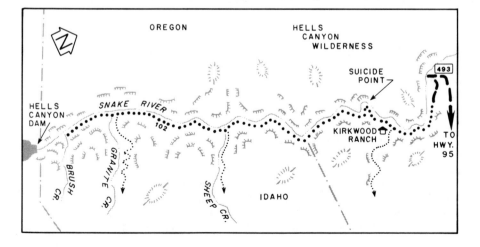

Rafting in Hells Canyon

Snake River in Hells Canyon

narrows, walls rise an incredible 8000 feet above the valley floor, and the river becomes a maelstrom tumbling from rapid to rapid. The actual end of the trail is 4 miles south of Granite Creek at Brush Creek, where boat transportation may be arranged (ahead of time) for the last couple of miles upriver to the road at Hells Canyon Dam. (For information on boat transportation by licensed operators, contact the Hells Canyon National Recreation Area office.)

The trip is recommended only for the spring and fall. From May on the worst problem is heat. If for some reason you do the trip then, carry plenty of water, several quarts per person per day, and hike early or late but never in midday.

To reach the trailhead, drive south from Lewiston on US 95 or north 28.4 miles from Riggins and then take a well-signed turn west to Pittsburg Landing. Parallel the Salmon River 1 mile and cross the bridge to the west side. Go left on Deer Creek road No. 493 (dirt) 17.6 miles, climbing to 4245-foot Pittsburg Saddle, then plunging to the Snake River. Near the canyon bottom the road splits. Take the left fork, very rough, past an old farmhouse and through the fields. In 0.7 bone-rattling mile the road ends at Upper Pittsburg Landing. The small camp area is a good place to park the car and walk the last 100 feet to the trailhead, elevation 1200 feet.

The trail, No. 102, is straightforward, requiring no directions. Watch carefully to avoid brushing against the poison ivy; read up on it before heading out. Rattlesnakes are active in the morning and evening and seek shade in the afternoon. Carry a long stick to shake clumps of grass ahead of you, and toss pebbles into shaded areas before entering them. A tent with doors that can be firmly closed at night permits sound sleep free from the fear of sharing your bag with a warmth-seeking snake.

The 5 up-and-down miles to the Kirkwood Living Historic Ranch give opportunities to meet challenges of the trail, overcome them, or retreat with dignity. The destination is fascinating in itself. The Forest Service maintains a museum (open June through August) in buildings of the old sheep ranch. Nearby are a moonshiner's cabin and the site of an Indian village. Several shaded hiker campsites have easy access to the river for a quick dip and to Kirkwood Creek for water. (When the museum is open, ask the staff for purified water from their outdoor tap.) Be sure to day-hike 3 miles beyond the ranch for the view from Suicide Point.

At 15 miles is Sheep Creek, where the canyon narrows. At 31 miles is Granite Creek, beyond which the trail dwindles to a meager path for the final 4 miles to Brush Creek. Beyond here is no trail, and the canyon walls are too steep for cross-country walking. Hikers must turn around or catch a boat up to the dam.

Suicide Point on Snake River trail

Mirror Lake and Tower of Babel

18 ▪ Seven Devils Loop

DAY HIKE	BACKPACK
Mirror Lake	**Seven Devils Loop**
Round trip • 6 miles	Loop trip • 25 miles
Hiking time • 5 hours	Hiking time • 4 days
High point • 7800 feet	High point • 8000 feet
Elevation gain • 900 feet in, 400 feet out	Elevation gain • 3100 feet

RESOURCES

Hikable • late June to mid-October
Management • Hells Canyon National Recreation Area
USGS map • He Devil
Hiker map • Hells Canyon National Recreation Area
Information • Riggins Office, Hells Canyon National Recreation Area, P.O. Box 832, Riggins, Idaho 83549; phone (208) 628-3916
Protection status • Hells Canyon Wilderness

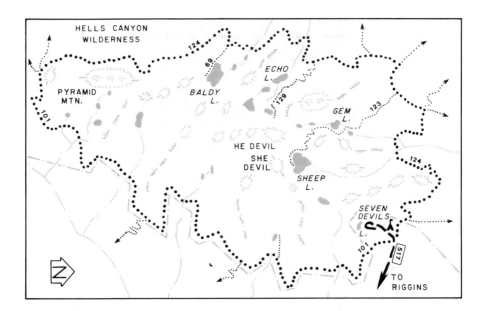

Craggy remnants of ancient volcanoes, snowcapped most of the summer, and some 40 cirque lakes set amid subalpine forest of pine, larch, spruce, and fir—all these several air-miles away and five life zones and 8000 feet above the Snake River, flowing through sagebrush and cactus and sun-hot rocks of the deepest canyon in the United States. The remoteness provides the solitude that gives a total of four qualities for greatness. The Seven Devils, whose name recalls the legendary ordeal of a lost Indian brave, are 9387-foot He Devil, the highest, and She Devil, Devils Tooth, Devils Thumb, Tower of Babel, the Ogre, and The Goblin. Lesser peaks have less ominous names.

Drive US 95 south of Lewiston to the town of Riggins. At 0.3 mile past the office of Hells Canyon National Recreation Area, turn west 17 miles on forest road No. 517 to Seven Devils Campground and trailhead, elevation 7500 feet.

The day hike samples the closest lake on a well-defined off-trail route. Find the unmarked path near the road-end. With a short bit of exposed scrambling, the way climbs a steep 900 feet over a saddle and descends scree to Mirror Lake, 7400 feet. Camping is possible.

For the loop, here described clockwise from the Seven Devils Campground, go left on trail No. 101, traversing the mostly dry east side of the range 11 miles and climbing to the ridge top near Horse Heaven Hill. Go north on trail No. 124, 4 miles, passing over an 8000-foot shoulder of Pyramid Mountain, past views, flower gardens, and Devils Farm, to Baldy Lake, 7190 feet. In 2 more miles from the lake is a junction. A 1-mile sidetrip on trail No. 129 leads to He Devil Lake beneath He Devil Mountain. The loop route continues 2 miles on trail No. 124 past Hibbs Cow Camp to a junction. For a second rewarding sidetrip, go east 3 miles (add 6 miles to total trip) on trail No. 123, passing Basin Lake and Gem Lake to Sheep Lake, 7875 feet.

Back on the loop trail, in ½ mile go right on trail No. 124 for 5 switchbacking miles, crossing an 8000-foot pass and descending to the starting point at Seven Devils Campground.

Northern California

The question might well be asked, why would any California hiker, with all the magnificence of the Sierra Nevada to roam, ever bother to visit the northern section of the state?

The answer lies partly in the somewhat better (so far) chance to be alone, population centers fairly distant, and most of the wildlands little-famed. However, the intrinsic beauties are their own reward. Popularity of redwood groves and ocean beaches needs no explanation, nor that of volcanoes. But there are also mild-mannered ridgelands to the west and sky-open desertlike ranges to the east in the South Warner Wilderness, and, in the Trinity Alps, peaks and valleys reminiscent of the North Cascades of Washington.

As elsewhere in California, summer weather is benign; the lower elevations appeal to hikers who have difficulty gaining sustenance from the thin air of the High Sierra.

Climbers do not find much solid rock of interest, but the lofty mass of Shasta offers stimulating challenges in winter and, on the glacier routes, good sport in any season.

In Redwood National Park and Prairie Creek Redwoods State Park, coast redwoods, some 20 feet in diameter and over 2000 years old, grouped in cathedral-like groves,

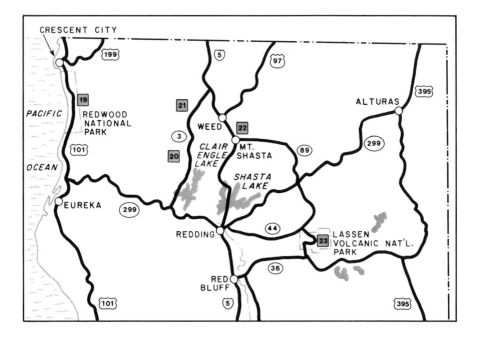

Bumpass Hell, Lassen Volcanic National Park

awe the most jaded traveler. Trails are short but numerous. Two favorites are the Miners Ridge trail and the Redwood Creek trail to the world's tallest tree, both in Hike 19.

High lakes, high passes, open forest, and broad flower fields are the attractions of the Trinity Alps Wilderness, on the south end of the Cascade Range: All are sampled on the wilderness traverse in Hike 20.

In the Marble Mountain Wilderness, miles of trails, including the Pacific Crest National Scenic Trail, or Pacific Crest Trail (PCT), which here follows the exact crest of the Cascade Range, give access to meadows and seventy-nine wilderness lakes (Hike 21).

Thousands of travelers on Interstate I-5 daily skirt the slopes of Mt. Shasta, which thus is the best-known Cascade volcano. Hike 22 up Black Butte gives a dramatic view of the monster mountain.

Boiling mudpots reminiscent of those in Yellowstone, a cinder cone, lava flows, and mountain lakes are a unique combination. Lassen Volcanic National Park's highlights are described in Hike 23.

19 ▪ World's Tallest Tree and the Miners Ridge–James Irvine Loop

DAY HIKE
World's Tallest Tree
One way • 8¹/₂ miles
Hiking time • 3 hours
High point • 262 feet
Elevation gain • 140 feet
Hikable • May to November

DAY HIKE OR BACKPACK
Miners Ridge–James Irvine Loop
Loop trip • 10 miles
Hiking time • 6 hours
High point • 560 feet
Elevation gain • 680 feet
Hikable • most of the year

RESOURCES

Management • Redwood National Park and Prairie Creek Redwoods State Park
USGS maps • Fern Canyon, Orick, Rodgers Peak
Hiker map • Redwood Map and Guide
Information • Redwood National Park; 111 2nd Street, Crescent City, California
    95531; phone (707) 464-6101
Protection status • Redwood National Park

An almost perpetual fog fills the redwood forest, masking the bubbling creeks and singing wrens, dimming the grazing elk and the ferns holding diamondlike droplets of water, and submerging tree tops. The experience of walking amongst groves of trees 300 feet tall, 20 feet in diameter, and over 2000 years old has been compared to visiting a Gothic cathedral.

The "great" requirements of virgin forest and abundant wildlife are emphatically met. The deficiencies in lakes and views are more than adequately compensated for by the Pacific Ocean and the awesome groves of trees.

Expect fog and rain throughout the year; carry a raincoat (and a tent if planning to spend the night). Remember that the year-round damp is essential for the existence of the coast redwood.

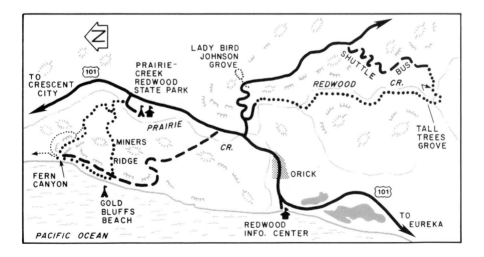

Miners Ridge trail

The world's tallest tree is located on Redwood Creek. This 600-year-old redwood, 367 feet tall and 14 feet in diameter, was discovered in 1963. Once accessible only by a 17-mile backpack, a Park Service shuttle bus makes it a ¹/₂-mile walk; stop by the visitors center in Orick for a bus schedule and other information. The trail is one of the best in the park and camping is allowed on some gravel bars. To enjoy both trail and trees, ride one way and hike the other. Both directions are equally comfortable, there being very little elevation gain or loss. Most people prefer to start at the lower end and hike the Redwood Creek trail upstream to the climax at the Tall Tree Grove.

The Miners Ridge–James Irvine Loop trail begins and ends in redwood forest. On the way the hiker passes through one cathedral-like grove after another, explores a magical canyon all atangle with delicate ferns, and strolls a sandy beach. Chances are very good of seeing elk, as well as deer and black bear.

Drive to the Prairie Creek Redwoods State Park Campground. (At the time of this writing, the campground was reached by driving US 101 south 31 miles from Crescent City or 46 miles north from Eureka. A bypass is being built around the state park so watch for signs indicating the Prairie Creek Redwoods State Park exit.) Park in the day-use area (fee charged), elevation 160 feet. Before doing anything else, tour the campground redwoods. Check out Elk Prairie, where a herd is in residence most of the year.

The hike begins from the trail sign in front of the visitors center. Following the nature loop, descend and cross a small creek, and then parallel it through a redwood grove. Two trails branch off on the right; the first leads to the Zig-Zag Trail and the second is the James Irvine Trail, the return leg of the loop.

After an easy 1/4 mile, the trail divides a third time. Go left and begin the moderately steep climb of the Miners Ridge Trail, a route once used by miners going from Prairie Creek to ocean-side camps at Gold Bluffs. A 1/2-mile sidetrail passed on the way loops by the site of an old miner's cabin. Attaining a maximum elevation of 560 feet, the trail begins a long, gentle descent to the coast.

In the forest at 4 miles is a hiker campsite (fee charged) with running water and a bear bar to hang your goodies at night. Just beyond the camp the trail ends at Gold Bluffs Beach Road. Directly across the road is Gold Bluffs Beach Campground, with beach access and solar-heated showers. The strip between bluffs and beach is home to a herd of elk; look for them in early morning and late afternoon, feeding on lupine and grass. Bears roam the beach and campground nightly; spot their tracks in the beach sand or perhaps at your tent door. (If they knock, improvise a back door.)

The loop heads right on road or beach north 2 miles to the road's end at Fern Canyon trailhead. Cross Home Creek (bridges are in place from late May to early September) and then follow the creek into Fern Canyon a spectacular 1/4 mile. The trail climbs out of the canyon to join the James Irvine Trail. Head east in redwood groves 4 1/4 miles to close the loop at the Prairie Creek Redwoods State Park Campground.

In the same area are several other excellent hikes. In Redwood National Park try the Damnation Trail, a 5-mile round trip through ancient forest to a sheltered ocean cove. The route begins at an unmarked turnout on US 101 at milepost 16 (this is south of Crescent City). A third fine choice is the Cathedral Trees–Rhododendron Trail Loop, a 6.5-mile celebration of redwoods, winding through groves, bending low to go under downed trees, and tunneling through burned-out tree trunks. The loop begins from Big Tree Wayside; ask at Prairie Creek Redwoods State Park for trail information.

Elk at Gold Beach

20 • Caribou Lake–Trinity Alps Traverse

SHORT BACKPACK	LONG BACKPACK
Caribou Lake	**Trinity Alps Traverse**
Round trip • 20 miles	One way • 40 miles with sidetrips
Hiking time • 2–3 days	Hiking time • 5–7 days
High point • 6822 feet	High point • 7600 feet
Elevation gain • 1700 feet	Elevation gain • 2900 feet
Hikable • late June through October	Hikable • July through October

RESOURCES

Management • Shasta and Trinity National Forests
USGS maps • Mt. Hilton, Thompson Peak, Siligo Peak
Hiker map • Forest Service's Trinity Alps Wilderness
Information • Weaverville Ranger District, P.O. Box T, Weaverville, California 96093; phone (916) 623-2121
Permits • Wilderness permit required
Protection status • Trinity Alps Wilderness

Scenery, flowers, forest, and lakes ringed by glacier-scoured rocks and permanent snowfields pass four of the six tests for greatness; wildlife is scattered and humanity abundant. Two exciting routes attain the high lakes of the Trinity Alps: the Stewart Fork (River) trail is a 17-mile wildflower walk from Stewart Campground to Sapphire Lake; described here is the shorter but more rugged trail from Coffee Creek to lovely Caribou Lake and a steep, rocky trail to Sapphire Lake that permits visiting both lakes from a single basecamp. By use of two cars, a one-way traverse gives the best of both routes. Neither of the two trails lend themselves to day hikes.

For the traverse, drive SR 3 north of Weaverville some 13 or 14 miles to a bridge across an inlet of Clair Engle Reservoir. Turn right on the Stewart Fork road and drive another 5 miles to the road-end and leave one car at the beginning of trail 9W20, elevation 2700 feet.

For Coffee Creek trail, drive SR 3 some 36 miles north of Weaverville or 67 miles

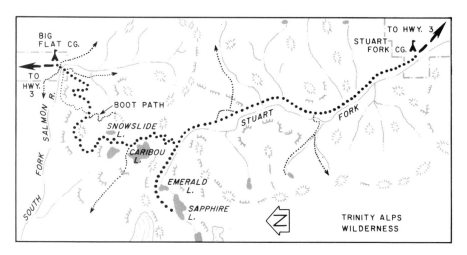

south of Yreka and turn west on the Coffee Creek road. Pass the Coffee Creek Ranger Station (pick up a wilderness permit) and drive almost 20 miles, crossing into the Salmon River watershed to Big Flats Campground and Caribou Lake trail No. 9W19, elevation 5200 feet.

The trail starts with a knee-deep ford of the South Fork Salmon River (if lucky, find a log) and then forks three ways (unsigned). Take the middle way and switchback up a brush-covered hillside with a scattering of magnificent pine trees 5 feet in diameter. In a scant mile continuous forest begins. The trail, a monotonous 10 percent grade with minor ups and downs, switchbacks to a 6200-foot ridge about 2 miles from Big Flats and enters a small meadow. In rollercoaster ups and downs of 200–300 feet, the way contours the side of Caribou Mountain. One ¼-mile stretch of tread is blasted across the face of a granite slab.

At 4½ miles pass Browns Meadow Camp near a gushing spring and switchback over a high shoulder, with views back to Mt. Shasta and forward to the huge snowfields on Thompson Peak and the rugged crest of the Sawtooth Range. At 9½ miles is Snow

Caribou Lake trail

Slide Lake, 6800 feet, the most popular lake in the Caribou Lake basin. At 10 miles reach Caribou Lake, 6822 feet.

From there a rough, steep trail climbs 3 miles over the 7600-foot crest of Sawtooth Ridge and drops 2600 feet to intersect Stewart Fork trail No. 9W20 at the 5000-foot level. Go right 1 mile to Emerald Lake, 5500 feet, and another 1 mile to Sapphire Lake, 5882 feet.

To complete the traverse, from Sapphire Lake follow the Stewart Fork trail 17 miles down through forest and famous flower fields, passing several good campsites. If a traverse is not intended, to avoid returning with a heavy pack up the steep trail from the Stewart Fork, do a day hike from Caribou Lake.

21 • Sky High Lakes–Sky High Traverse

DAY HIKE OR BACKPACK
Sky High Lakes
Round trip • 14 miles (18 miles for
  loop)
Hiking time • 8 hours (2 days for loop)
High point • 5800 feet (6500 feet for
  loop)
Elevation gain • 1500 feet (2200 feet for
  loop)

BACKPACK
Sky High Traverse
Round trip • 30 miles
Hiking time • 4 days
High point • 6600 feet
Elevation gain • 4000 feet in, 2000 feet
  out

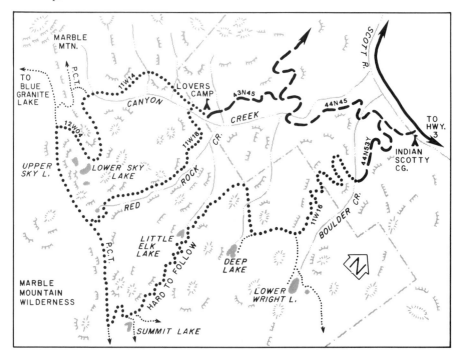

Sky High Lakes Basin

RESOURCES
Hikable • mid-June through September
Management • Klamath National Forest
USGS maps • Boulder Peak, Marble Mtn., Ukonom Lake
Hiker map • Marble Mountain Wilderness
Information • Scott River Ranger District, Fort Jones, California 96032; phone (916)
    468-5351
Permits • Permit needed for campfires
Protection status • Marble Mountain Wilderness

For any fan of mountain lakes, the seventy-nine such in the Marble Mountain Wilderness guarantee a great hike. In addition there are pleasant forests, great wildflowers, and ridge-top meadows and miles of views. The wilderness is traversed by the Pacific Crest National Scenic Trail (PCT), which gives access to a baker's dozen of the most beautiful lakes. Some can be sampled on a strenuous day hike or a two-day loop. However, the traverse requires a full week to soak in the essence of the lake basins and high ridges.

A sampling can be made on either a day hike to Sky High Lakes Basin or a two- to three-day loop up Red Rock Valley, returning by way of the lakes and Marble Valley, mixing together forest, flower-covered meadows, panoramic views, and alpine lakes.

From Yreka drive SR 3 to Fort Jones, turn right on narrow, twisty Scott River road 14 miles to Indian Scotty Campground, and turn left on forest road No. 44N45. For the day-hike sampler, drive 5.4 miles and turn left 2 more miles on 43N45 to the road-end at Lovers Camp. Pass the horse camp and park at the hikers' campground and Marble Valley Trail No. 11W14, elevation 4200 feet.

Follow a path into the forest and in 1000 feet meet a logging road and go left, descending a bit to the true trail. In a little over $^1/_2$ mile is a junction.

For the direct route to the lakes stay right on the Marble Valley trail. With numerous ups (some very steep) and downs (also steep), in $5^1/_2$ miles pass the white wall that has given the name to the valley and wilderness. Keep left at a junction and climb another $^1/_2$ mile up a steep hillside to the large meadow with the three Sky High Lakes.

For the recommended loop, at the first junction, go left on the Red Rock Valley trail No. 11W18. This clockwise looping is best because the grade is gentler and when coming the other way some of the trail junctions are hard to spot. From the junction at $^1/_2$ mile, the Red Rock Valley trail crosses into the Red Rock watershed and alternates between cool forest and large green meadows, flower-covered in season. The way is easy to lose at creek crossings, so be watchful and check the map carefully. Along the way are several good campsites. At approximately 7 miles reach the ridge top, 6300 feet. Go right on the PCT, alternating between forest, brush, and big meadows approximately 3 miles to a trail junction. Go right on trail No. 12W04 and in a few feet right again, descending 1 mile to campsites at Sky High Lakes and 7 more miles back to Lovers Camp on the Marble Valley Trail.

For the backpack, the Sky High Traverse, drive Scott River road to Indian Scotty Campground and turn left on forest road No. 44N45 for 1.4 miles and left again on road No. 44N53Y to the road-end at the Boulder Creek trailhead, elevation 3800 feet.

Hike $1^1/_2$ miles on trail No. 11W16 to a junction; perhaps take a $1^1/_2$-mile sidetrip to 6900-foot Lower Wright Lake. For the Sky High Lakes, stay right, passing Deep Lake, 6300 feet, and drop a bit to Little Elk Lake, 5400 feet, and a junction at 5 miles. Go left on a poor trail and climb steep, short switchbacks over a 6300-foot ridge and drop to Summit Lake, 6000 feet, 10 miles from the road. The trail improves and intersects the PCT at 1 mile, 6596 feet. Follow the PCT west through trees and meadows 4 miles and turn right, descending to Sky High Valley and Sky High Lakes, 5800 feet, 15 miles from the road.

Most hikers are content with this scene but others are tantalized by the existence of more lakes, more meadows, and more to see. For the more, continue on the PCT another 8 miles, following ridge tops, traversing the south side of Marble Mountain, 6990 feet, and the side of 6500-foot Pigeon Roost to a junction and several options, all great. The right fork leads 5 miles to three Granite Lakes—Green Granite, Gold Granite, and Blue Granite—and also to Ukonom Lake, largest in the wilderness. The left fork goes $^1/_2$ mile to Cuddihy Lakes, and the straight-ahead leads out on Sandy Ridge for more views.

Western anemone

22 ▪ Black Butte–Mount Shasta Loop

DAY HIKE
Black Butte
Round trip • 5 miles
Hiking time • 4 hours
High point • 6325 feet
Elevation gain • 1800 feet

BACKPACK
Mount Shasta Loop
Under construction

RESOURCES

Hikable • June through October
Management • Shasta National Forest
USGS map • City of Mount Shasta
Hiker map • None
Information • Shasta National Forest, Mount Shasta, California 96067; phone (916)
    926-4511
Protection status • Mount Shasta Wilderness

Shasta ranks with Mt. Rainier as one of the two most massive volcanoes in the mainland United States and is the nation's hugest free-standing peak close beside an interstate highway. Unfortunately, logging roads have eliminated most trails and so shortened the others that none qualifies as great. However, in 1984 the upper reaches of the peak were designated as wilderness and it is hoped the around-the-mountain trail now being constructed will deserve the "great" distinction. At present we recommend a short, steep climb up an extinct cinder cone to a spectacular view of Mt. Shasta. When the eyes can be pried loose from that, there also are views far out to the Trinity Alps, farms, and cities and far down to I-5 and the Southern Pacific Railroad, where toy cars and trucks and miniature trains creep in their petty pace this way and that.

Drive I-5 to the Mount Shasta City exit. In the city center at the corner of Mt. Shasta Boulevard and East Lake Street, head uphill toward Mt. Shasta. The road curves left, passes a playfield and a school, and climbs to timberline. At 2.7 miles from Mt.

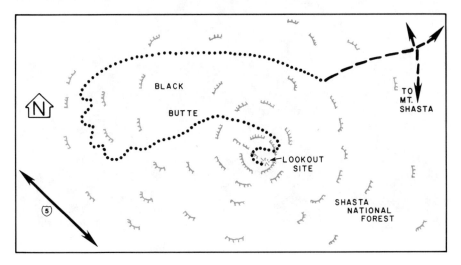

Shasta Boulevard go left on a dirt road that usually is signed "Black Butte Trail." At 1.7 miles from the pavement, turn right 2.7 miles to a four-way intersection. Turn left 0.6 mile to the road-end on the northeast corner of Black Butte. Very limited parking, elevation 4400 feet.

The trail starts in forest shade on tread spread with crushed rock. Openings in the trees begin, giving views to the north. The way sidehills up around the north side of the butte to the west side directly above I-5. At about $1^1/_2$ miles it switchbacks and crosses a rugged boulder field and then swings back around the north side to the east side and the big views of Shasta. Switchbacks up a rocky slope culminate in the rounded summit. Getting to the foundation of the old lookout demands some hairy rock scrambling; be content with the view a few feet lower. What a view it is! Mt. Eddy to the west, Castle Crags south, Mt. Shasta east, and, off in the distance, in Oregon, Mt. McLoughlin.

Mount Shasta from Black Butte trail

23 ▪ Lassen Peak, Bumpass Hell, and the Cinder Cone–Horseshoe Lake Loop

DAY HIKE
Bumpass Hell
Round trip • 3 miles
Hiking time • 2 hours
High point • 8500 feet
Elevation gain • 300 feet in, 400 feet
out

DAY HIKE
Lassen Peak
Loop trip • 5 miles
Hiking time • 4 hours
High point • 10,457 feet
Elevation gain • 2000 feet

ONE DAY OR BACKPACK
Cinder Cone–Horseshoe Lake Loop
Loop trip • 18 miles
Hiking time • 10 hours
High point • 7000 feet
Elevation gain • 2500 feet

RESOURCES

Hikable • mid-July through October
Management • Lassen Volcanic National Park
USGS map • Lassen Volcanic National Park, special edition
Hiker map • Hikers Map and Guide to Lassen Volcanic Park
Information • Lassen Volcanic National Park, P.O. Box 100, Mineral, California
96063; phone (916) 595-4444
Permits • Backcountry permits required for camping
Protection status • Lassen Volcanic National Park

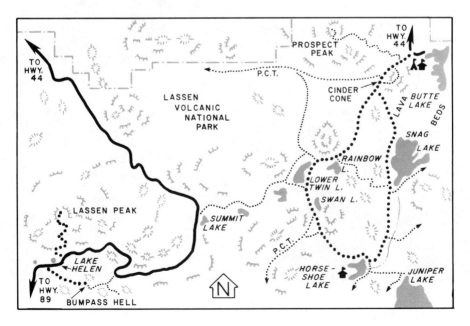

Mount Lassen climaxed its modern activity in 1915, when the top of the mountain blew off sideways. Boiling mudpots and steaming hot springs are the central attractions of the short sampler walk to Bumpass Hell; an added dividend in late July and early August is wildflowers. A long volcanic history is delineated by a fascinating variety of features: impenetrable lava flows, multicolored cinder cones, and bubbling hot springs.

Fantastic Lava Beds and Snag Lake

Not to be overlooked is the ascent of 10,457-foot Lassen Peak, to the site of the lookout building that was brandnew when it was blown to smithereens in the 1915 eruption.

For the day hikes, drive the Lassen Volcanic National Park road to Helen Lake from either the south or west entrance. The Bumpass Hell trailhead is located just below the lake, elevation 8200 feet, and the Lassen Peak trail at 1 mile above Helen Lake, elevation 8500 feet.

The Bumpass Hell trail carries throngs of visitors through alpine meadows to an 8500-foot high point and then descends. In a little over 1 mile, at the first switchback, is a common turnaround point at an excellent view of the scene that Mr. Bumpass thought looked like Hell. At 1 1/2 miles are the hot springs; the soil is very fragile so stay on the boardwalks.

The Lassen Peak trail, wide and steep, starts at the upper limits of vegetation and switchbacks 2 1/2 miles up volcanic rubble, often covered with snow, to the summit. Carry plenty of clothing. The air may be balmy at the trailhead, windy and freezing on top. Take your time; the elevation gain is not great but the air is noticeably thin at 10,000 feet.

The longer hike, the Cinder Cone–Horseshoe Lake Loop, tours cinder cones and skirts lava flows, with six mountain lakes thrown in. The trip can be done in a single long day—and long it truly is, what with so much of the way being through soft cinder, as tiring as soft snow. An overnighter is less strenuous. There are no formal campsites and the only restrictions are to camp 100 feet from water or a trail and build no wood fires.

Drive SR 44 east 11 miles from the junction with SR 89 or 41 miles west from Susanville and turn south 6 dusty miles to the road-end at Butte Lake, elevation 6100 feet.

The trail leaves the day-use area near the terminus of an old lava flow and heads west on the route of Nobel's Emigrant Trail. In 1 mile is a junction. The left fork steeply climbs more than 500 feet to the top of Cinder Cone and down the other side to rejoin the main trail.

The summit must be visited, offering as it does the broadest and most intriguing views of vulcanism. However, the path is steep and the soft cinder tiring. Backpackers usually prefer not to take the left fork but to stay on the lower trail around the west side of the cone, drop packs, and climb the far side unloaded. Whichever ascent route is taken, circle the 1/4-mile crater, explore down in the crater, and look east to the Fantastic Lava Beds and Painted Dunes, north to Butte Lake, south to Snag Lake, and off to the west to Lassen Peak.

Emigrants in the 1850s testified that Cinder Cone was active when they passed, but scientists say the last eruption was 1500 years ago. What do you think? Did it really erupt or just give the appearance of steaming? Blowing dust, maybe? Hysterical emigrants?

From the cone the trail crosses a corner of the Painted Dunes to the Snag Lake trail, which leads to the lake, 6076 feet, 4 1/2 miles from the road-end, counting the sidetrip up Cinder Cone. Round the shore 1 1/2 miles to a junction. The right fork offers a shorter loop but the recommended route is along the lake and then Grassy Creek, 3 miles to Horseshoe Lake, 6700 feet. From here go right 3 miles, crossing a 7000-foot high point below Crater Butte to the narrow neck dividing Upper Twin Lake and go right, climbing a scant mile to Rainbow Lake and proceeding 5 miles back to the road-end at Butte Lake. (Note that a new trail connects Butte Lake to Triangle Lake and a dozen or more others in the adjacent Caribou Wilderness.)

OREGON

The Oregon Cascades, entirely volcanic in origin, offer the climber nothing more exciting than snowfields, a few small glaciers, and rotten rock. Furthermore, located in one of the world's most prolific and high-profit tree-growing zones, the range retains the merest scraps of pristine valley forest. Hiking is confined to subalpine forests, parklands, and meadows. The Wallowa Mountains have much sounder rock but the cliff dimensions are too small for more than minor challenges. However, the range contains the largest alpine area in the state, a geological and ecological hybrid of the High Sierra and North Cascades and Colorado Rockies that provides unique variety to the wilderness backpacker. Other Oregon areas, at elevations from sea level to volcanic-crag level, are strictly for walking or floating.

Oregon's national wildernesses are generally tiny and the total acreage sadly inadequate, but the number of preserves (twelve) is impressive, each guarding one or another special treasure. Happily, the domination of the public lands by commodity extractors at long last has engendered one of the nation's most vigorous environmental communities, and one with strong support from the public. The prognosis for additional wilderness is excellent.

(Space limitation forced the exclusion of the trail to Green Lake in the Three Sisters Wilderness and the miles of sand dunes in Oregon Dunes National Recreation Area.)

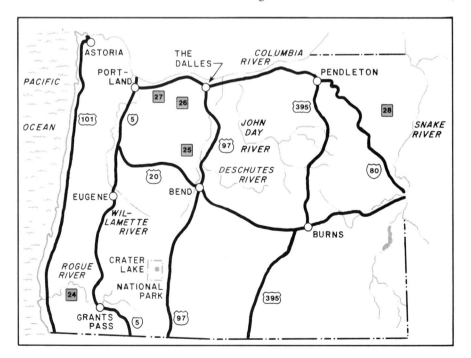

Ramona Falls, Mount Hood Wilderness

West Fork Wallowa River near Frazer Lake, Eagle Cap Wilderness

The wild and scenic Rogue River in the Wild Rogue Wilderness of southern Oregon is one of the most popular rafting rivers in the Northwest. Less known and less crowded is the forested Rogue River trail (Hike 24), which follows the river.

The Mount Jefferson Wilderness is a popular wilderness on the crest of the Oregon Cascades with snowfields, a glacier-white volcano, forests, lakes, and alpine meadows. Many highlights can be reached on a day hike, and all can be savored in the week-long trip of Hike 25.

In the Mount Hood Wilderness, the Timberline Trail (Hike 26) is a grand loop around Oregon's highest mountain, traversing alpine meadows and forests, crossing raging torrents, and skirting glaciers.

The Columbia Gorge National Scenic Area offers a gorge carved through the Cascade Range by the Columbia River with the Northwest's most famous waterfalls. Some can be viewed from a car window but the best are reached in Hike 27.

Glacier-polished granite, alpine lakes, vast flower-covered meadows, streams, and forests demand that the Eagle Cap Wilderness be explored. Trails to lakes with fish are crowded; other stretches of the Glacier Lake Loop (Hike 28) are seldom trod.

24 • Rogue River

DAY HIKE	BACKPACK
Flora Dell Falls	**Rogue River Trail**
Round trip • 9 miles	One way • 40 miles
Hiking time • 5 hours	Hiking time • 5 days
High point • 500 feet	High point • 689 feet
Elevation gain • 50 feet	Elevation gain • 200 feet

RESOURCES

Hikable • year-round
Management • Siskiyou National Forest
USGS maps • Agness, Marial, Galice
Hiker maps • Siskiyou National Forest maps and Wild & Scenic Rogue River maps
Information • Forest Supervisor, Siskiyou National Forest, P.O. Box 440, Grants Pass, Oregon 97526; phone (503) 479-5301
Protection status • Wild Rogue Wilderness

The wild and scenic Rogue is among the most renowned rafting rivers in the Northwest. However, riding the surface of the waters is a different experience from hiking beside noisy rapids or looking down tall cliffs to the water. To appreciate why the Rogue is a great hike, do both. The water and the forests suffice for a great hike; because most visitors ride rafts, the trail offers a surprising degree of solitude. Wildlife is abundant,

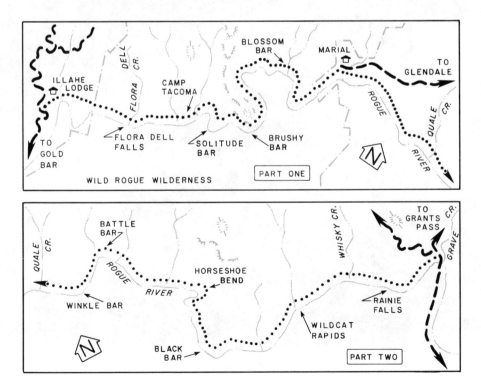

including bears; hang packs out of reach. The trail can be hiked from the upper end, reached from Grants Pass on I-5 or, as described here, from the lower end, reached from Gold Bar on US 101. A one-way trip will require a second car or other arrangements.

From Gold Bar drive the south side of the Rogue 31 miles. Cross the river, immediately turn right, and continue upstream 4 miles to the trailhead at Illahe, elevation 474 feet.

Rogue River trail No. 1160 skirts Illahe Lodge (to stay at this and the other private lodges, advance reservations are necessary), passes Billings Creek, and at 1 mile enters the Wild Rogue Wilderness. At 4 1/2 miles is the beautiful waterfall at Flora Dell Creek, a good turnaround for a day-hike sampler.

At 6 miles is Clay Hill Creek Lodge and in a scant 1 mile more, Camp Tacoma near Tate Creek; here are tentsites. At 8 miles is Solitude Bar, which offered anything but solitude in 1900, when the bar was a busy mine. Piles of rubble can still be found above the trail. A mile farther is Bushy Bar, another turn-of-the-century mining scene.

More campsites are at Blossom Bar, 13 miles, site of a stampmill that crushed ore. The river enters a narrow canyon where hikers may be entertained watching rafters come bouncing through. At 16 miles the way leaves the wilderness at the community of Marial,

Rafting the Rogue River

reached by a tortuous forest road. Walk the road through the town past Rogue River Ranch, built about 1880 (the present buildings date from about 1903), to campsites at East Mule Creek. At Winkle Bar, 22 miles, pass the log cabin once owned by Zane Grey. Numerous campsites in the next 12 miles permit a flexible, relaxed schedule. At 34 miles gold was discovered across the river in 1851; evidence of the digging remains. At 37 miles, near Whiskey Creek, is a miner's cabin built in 1880. The two segments of Rainie Falls are at 38 miles; the lower one forces rafters to portage. At 40 miles the trail ends at Grave Creek on the Rogue River some 24 miles from I-5.

25 • Mount Jefferson Wilderness Traverse

DAY HIKE	BACKPACK
Jefferson Park	**Wilderness Traverse**
Round trip • 12 miles	Round trip • 60 miles
Hiking time • 7 hours	Hiking time • 7 days
High point • 7000 feet	High point • 7000 feet
Elevation gain • 1500 feet in, 1200 feet out	Elevation gain • 8100 feet

RESOURCES

Hikable • July to late October
Management • Willamette National Forest
USGS maps • Mt. Jefferson, Breitenbush Hot Springs
Hiker map • Mt. Jefferson Wilderness
Information • Detroit Ranger Station, Star Route Box 320, Mill City, Oregon 97360; phone (503) 854-3360
Protection status • Mount Jefferson Wilderness
Permits • Forest Service permit needed for overnight trips

Jefferson Park is considered by many Oregonians to be the most beautiful corner of the state, a veritable paradise, and lots of folks who don't think of themselves as hikers undertake a trail pilgrimage to lay eyes on the broad meadow, its little lake, and the lava-craggy and glacier-white heap of 10,498-foot Mt. Jefferson. That's the day-hike

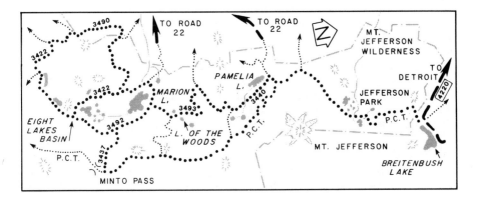

Mount Jefferson from Park Ridge

sampler. The wilderness traverse adds much more, including a cluster of lakes beneath the rough summit of 7841-foot Three Fingered Jack, the eroded remnants of an ancient volcano.

There is a shorter way to the highlights via the Whitewater forest road, but for the best views, go as described here. From Albany drive SR 22 west to the town of Detroit. Turn left on the Breitenbush River road, which becomes forest road No. 46. Just short of 17 miles go left on road No. 4220; in 1 mile the way deteriorates and the last 5 miles are a rude track built in the 1930s for Model A's. (The alternative is a 17-mile detour by way of Lake Olallie; the last 5 miles may be no better.) At Breitenbush Lake find the crossing of the Pacific Crest National Scenic Trail (PCT), elevation 5500 feet.

Head south from the lake on the PCT, going up and down on the forested bumps and dips of a broad ridge. In 3³/₄ miles the trail climbs meadows to a 7000-foot high point near the top of Park Ridge. The view to Jefferson Park makes a person agree with the Oregonians. It surely does look like Paradise ought to look. The trail drops to the park and to camps near Scout Lake, 5856 feet, 6 miles from the Breitenbush road.

The backpack traverse follows the PCT south 5 miles, losing 1600 feet to Woodpecker Ridge, then a long 6 miles climbing 2400 feet into meadows at the 6000-foot level below Cathedral Rocks. The way reaches the crest of the Cascade Mountains and stays high for 5 miles, sometimes in flowers, sometimes in trees, always in views either east or west, to Minto Pass. Here, leave the PCT and go right on trail No. 3437, descending forest in the direction of Marion Lake. At 2³/₄ miles go left on trail No. 3492 another 3¹/₂ miles to meadows in Eight Lakes Basin, 5100 feet, 32 miles from Breitenbush Lake. Seven of the lakes are tree-ringed; Jorn Lake has excellent meadow views of Three Fingered Jack.

Two return routes may be taken to Breitenbush Lake: The first is 29 miles via trail No. 3422 some 4 miles to Marion Lake, then 13 miles on trails No. 3493 and No. 3440 to Pamelia Lake, another ¹/₅ mile to a junction with the PCT, and a final 12 miles to the starting point. The second is a 40-mile route with more lakes, and more trees and streams. For this, go south 1 mile on trail No. 3422, gaining 300 feet to tiny Alice Lake in a pass between Three Fingered Jack and Red Butte. Keep on trail No. 3422 another 1³/₄ mile, descending into woods past Mowich Lake and Duffy Lake to a junction. Go right on trail No. 3427 along the North Santiam River 2 miles, then right 6 miles on trail No. 3490. Cross the river (just a stream), then Swede Creek, leave the wilderness for 2 miles as the trail rounds the west side of Turpentine Peak to roaded Pine Ridge Lake, go right on trail No. 3443, cross Pine Ridge, and return to wilderness. Descend 4¹/₂ miles past Temple Lake to trail No. 3422 and Marion Lake. From here follow the Pamelia Lake trail back to Breitenbush Lake as described above.

Heart-leaved arnica

26 ▪ Cooper Spur–Timberline Trail

DAY HIKE
Cooper Spur
Round trip • 6 miles
Hiking time • 5 hours
High point • 8500 feet
Elevation gain • 2500 feet

BACKPACK
Timberline Trail
Loop trip • 40$^1/_2$ miles
Hiking time • 5 days
High point • 7320 feet
Elevation gain • 8600 feet

RESOURCES

Hikable • August and September
Management • Mount Hood National Forest
USGS maps • Mt. Hood South, Mt. Hood North–Government Camp, Bull Run Lake
Hiker map • Mt. Hood Wilderness
Information • Zigzag Ranger District, Zigzag, Oregon 97049; phone (503) 666-0704
Protection status • Mount Hood Wilderness
Permits • Forest Service permit needed for overnight trips

Satisfying four of the six criteria for a great hike, the Timberline Trail around Mt. Hood is a circuit second in the Northwest only to the Wonderland Trail around Mt. Rainier, ranging from alpine meadows rich in wildflowers to forested valleys with raging streams muddied by glaciers. Historical interest is added by stone shelters built by the Civilian Conservation Corps in the 1930s. What with around-the-mountain backpackers, plus day-hikers setting out from the numerous roads that extend up flanks of the mountain, during the brief six weeks between snow seasons the trail is thronged.

Warning: The route traverses several permanent snowfields and, at least through mid-August, temporary snowpatches that may be easy to cross on hot afternoons but can be ice-hard in cloudy weather or early morning. The ranger recommends carrying

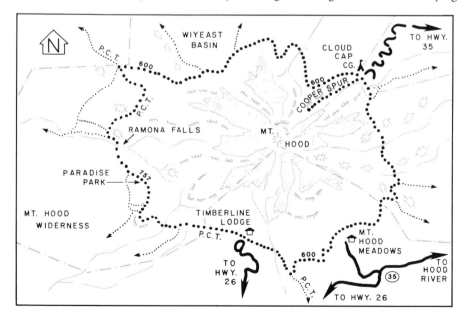

Mount Hood from Cloud Cap Inn

ski poles or an ice ax. Additionally, six or more muddy torrents must be forded, safe enough in midsummer, but usually not with dry feet.

The Timberline Trail can be sampled from any of the half-dozen roads to the wilderness boundary, including the road to Cloud Cap Inn where the recommended day hike begins (directions given later).

For the Timberline Trail, drive US 26 east of Portland to Government Camp and turn left to Timberline Lodge, elevation 5900 feet, on the south side of Mt. Hood.

Walk a paved trail uphill a few hundred feet from the lodge to the Pacific Crest National Scenic Trail (PCT)/Timberline Trail. The loop is described here clockwise but counterclockwise is just as good; take your choice. Heading west, the trail passes chairlifts, a radio relay station, and numerous tourists, most of whom are left behind at 1 mile where the way crosses Little Zigzag Canyon. At 2 miles is a view into the canyon and then a descent to the Zigzag River at 4900 feet, the first difficult crossing. The trail switchbacks up to lower gardens of Paradise Park at 5800 feet, 5 miles from Timberline Lodge.

The trail loses 3000 feet in numerous switchbacks to a ford of Sandy River at 9 miles; 1/2 mile beyond are Ramona Falls and excellent campsites. The trail descent continues to the route's lowest point, 2810 feet, and a ford of the wide, braided Muddy Fork, 11 1/2 miles from Timberline Lodge. The way then regains the lost elevation. At 13 1/2 miles the PCT leaves the Mount Hood Wilderness and heads north. Timberline Trail climbs Bald Ridge, passing a view of Sandy Glacier, to a 5400-foot high point

Timberline Trail on side of Cooper Spur, Mount Adams in distance

under McNeil Point and contours up and down, the views of ice and rock magnificent, through Cairn Basin, Eden Park, and Wy East Basin to Elk Cove, 20^1/$_2$ miles from Timberline Lodge. The way drops 200 feet into Cole Canyon and climbs over 5800-foot Stranahan Ridge to a crossing of Eliot Creek on a bridge, coming to Cloud Cap Campground at 25 miles.

Nearby is the century-old Cloud Cap Inn, now used as a rescue center and not open to the public. The inn is reached from SR 35 out of Hood River. A paved road leads to Cooper Spur Ski Area; forest road No. 3512 continues to Cloud Cap Inn and Campground.

The campground is the base for a recommended day hike, or "rest day" sidetrip for backpackers. The well-graded trail ascending to the 8500-foot level of Cooper Spur gives dramatic views into crevasses of Eliot Glacier, largest in Oregon, and out to giant volcanoes of southern Washington and northern Oregon. Hike the Timberline Trail uphill 1 mile, turn right on the Cooper Spur Trail past the newly reconstructed Cooper Spur Hut, and, after many switchbacks, attain the viewpoint and the high camp used by summit climbers.

Back at Cloud Cap Campground, don't mistake an unmarked moraine trail for the Timberline Trail, which is delineated by large cairns. It ascends barren slopes of Cooper Spur to the route's highest point, 7320 feet, crossing what may be difficult snowfields before descending to more hospitable terrain below Lamberson Butte and Gnarl Ridge, 3 miles from Cloud Cap.

In the next 10 miles the trail ducks in and out of numerous ravines, sometimes in forest, sometimes in volcanic rubble. It passes beneath ski lifts at Mt. Hood Meadows, drops to a ford of White River at 4800 feet, intersects the PCT coming in from the south, and ascends a narrow ridge to a crossing of the Salmon River. At 40 miles it returns to the starting point at Timberline Lodge.

27 • Columbia Gorge Trails

DAY HIKE	DAY HIKE OR BACKPACK
Wahkeena–Multnomah Falls Loop	**Eagle Punch Bowl–Texas Camp**

Loop trip • 5 miles
Hiking time • 3 hours
High point • 1400 feet
Elevation gain • 1000 feet

Round trip to Eagle Punch Bowl • 3¹/₂
  miles
Hiking time • 2 hours
Round trip to Texas Camp • 15 miles
Hiking time • 7 hours
High point • 1100 feet
Elevation gain • 400 feet

RESOURCES

Hikable • most of the year
Management • Columbia River Gorge National Scenic Area
USGS map • Bonneville Dam 15-minute
Hiker map • Forest Trails of the Columbia Gorge
Information • Columbia Gorge Ranger Station, 31520 S.E. Woodard Road, Troutdale,
    Oregon 97230; phone (503) 695-2276
Protection status • Columbia Gorge National Scenic Area

The Oregon side of the Columbia Gorge is famous for waterfalls. Some of the most beautiful can be glimpsed from the windows of moving cars, but the best views—and many of the falls—only can be seen from trails. Though the gorge is one of the grandest natural wonders and hiking certainly is the supreme experience of the scene, no single existing trail so outranks the others as to be called "the greatest." Frankly, deficiencies in wildlife and flowers and solitude would make the scene only marginally great were it not for the waterfalls, so spectacular they richly compensate for other lacks. Volunteers are working on a 200-mile loop along the rim of the gorge that surely will be rated world-class.

From Portland drive I-80N eastward. At Bridal Valley, Exit 28 (eastbound only), go off the freeway onto the Scenic Highway (westbound, use Exit 35).

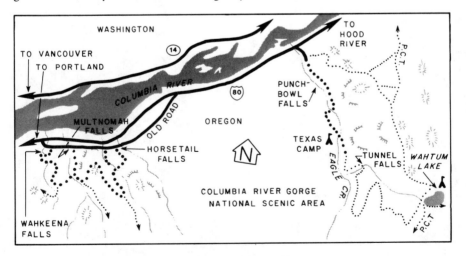

The first stop is for a 3¹/₂-mile loop trail (climbing about 700 feet) or a 5-mile loop (gaining about 1000 feet). Both go by 242-foot-high Wahkeena Falls and 611-foot-high Multnomah Falls.

From the small parking lot below Wahkeena Falls, find trail No. 420, cross Wahkeena Creek, and after a long switchback recross just below the falls. At ¹/₂ mile is a junction. For the short loop go straight ahead on trail No. 421, contouring past viewpoints to a crossing of Multnomah Creek. For the long loop go right, climbing within sound of Wahkeena Creek and more waterfalls, then contouring left on trail No. 419 past viewpoints of the Columbia Gorge to a junction near Multnomah Creek. Descend on trail No. 441 to an intersection with the short loop and take a short spur to the lip of Multnomah Falls. Retrace steps to the intersection, descend under Multnomah Falls to the visitor lodge, and return on trail No. 442 to the starting point via a trail a short distance above the road.

An alternative to the loop trips is the spectacular mile-long paved trail from the bottom of Multnomah Falls to the top. Falls-watching competes with tourist-watching.

For more hikes, continue on the Scenic Highway 2.3 miles beyond Multnomah Falls to Oneonta Creek. In late summer when the water is low, the narrow defile can be walked and waded ¹/₂ mile upstream.

Drive another 0.3 mile to Horsetail Falls. Take trail No. 438 a steep ³/₄ mile to a viewpoint of the Columbia River and pass behind upper Horsetail Falls, a singularly impressive curtain of water when viewed from a dry passageway on the backside.

The Eagle Creek trail, the longest trail and the only one suitable for a backpack, follows Eagle Creek through forest and across the face of cliffs, passing the lovely and much-photographed Eagle Creek Punch Bowl, to campsites in the woods.

This trailhead can *only* be reached from the eastbound lane of I-80N. Take Exit 41, the first after Bonneville, go past Eagle Creek Fish Hatchery to the road-end, and walk the Eagle Creek trail No. 440 upstream. At 1³/₄ miles turn right, descending very steeply to the Punch Bowl. For more trees and camping and less people, regain the trail and continue upstream. At 2¹/₂ miles the path makes a sharp horseshoe bend and crosses a small stream on a steel bridge. At 3¹/₂ miles is a high bridge over Eagle Creek. A short distance beyond are campsites at Texas Camp. In the next 4 miles the trail passes waterfalls and more campsites ending at a road near Wahtum Lake.

Opposite: *Multnomah Falls.* Above: *Eagle Creek Punch Bowl*

28 • Glacier Lake Loop

DAY HIKE	BACKPACK
None	**Glacier Lake Loop**
	Loop trip • 35 miles
	Hiking time • 5 days
	High point • 8800 feet
	Elevation gain • 4200 feet

RESOURCES

Hikable • mid-July through October
Management • Wallowa–Whitman National Forest
USGS maps • Joseph, Eagle Cap
Hiker map • Forest Service's Eagle Cap Wilderness
Information • Wallowa Valley Ranger District, Rt. 1 Box 83, Joseph, Oregon 97846;
    phone (503) 432-2171
Protection status • Eagle Cap Wilderness

Alpine lakes in glacier-scoured basins compete for attention with wildflowers and snowcapped mountains. Add in the forests and four of the six criteria for a great hike are satisfied. As for the other two, the enormous parking lot for hikers' cars and the several establishments of horse outfitters at the trailhead give due warning that the lakes get far more human attention than is good for them and consequently little animal attention. The trip described here is a 35-mile loop that visits the overcrowded lakes and also a more lonesome area famed for wildflowers. Glacier Lake also can be done as a shorter 25$\frac{1}{2}$-mile round trip.

Drive I-84 to LaGrande and go left (east) on SR 82 to Enterprise. Continue 12 miles through Joseph and around the east side of Wallowa Lake to the inlet. Go left, avoiding the state park and pass the miniature golf course, pony rides, and pack outfitters to the road-end and trailhead, elevation 1800 feet.

In 150 feet the trail splits. For the short trail to Glacier Lake, keep right, circling

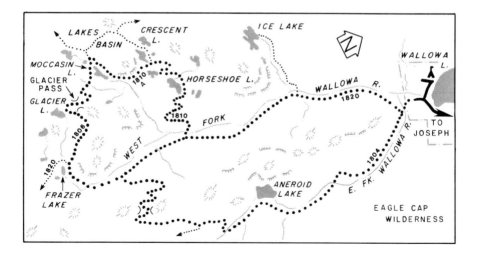

Glacier Lake

above a powerhouse, and follow the West Fork Wallowa River trail No. 1820 upstream. For the recommended loop, go left on trail No. 1804 and follow the East Fork Wallowa River 6 miles to Aneroid Lake, 7500 feet. From the lake the trail climbs into flower fields where the trail is easily lost in lush greenery. Keep right at the first junction and keep right again at the next junction and follow trail No. 1831 and upward to sparse arctic-tundra vegetation. The way attains an 8800-foot high point before dropping to the West Fork Wallowa River trail No. 1820, some 8 miles from Aneroid Lake. In $1^1/_2$ miles the West Fork trail leads upstream through a narrowing valley to alpine meadows and Frazier Lake, 7150 feet. The path, now trail No. 1806, remains in meadows upstream along the river (now a creek) 2 more miles to Glacier Lake, 8200 feet. Seek out a private campsite as far as possible from the madding crowd and spend several days exploring other lakes and climbing trail No. 1805 to the summit of 9595-foot Eagle Cap.

From Glacier Lake the loop route heads for Lake Basin, a group of seven lakes in glacier-scooped bowls. The trail crosses 8500-foot Glacier Pass and in 3 miles reaches Moccasin Lake, 7600 feet, the first of the too-popular Basin Lakes. Follow trail No. 1810A northward until it joins trail No. 1810. The way weaves around five of the lakes before dropping to the West Fork trail No. 1820, some 6 miles from the road-end.

This backpack is an unsurpassed introduction to scenery of the Wallowa Mountains, which remind a person of both the High Sierra and the North Cascades. A lot more scenery in the wilderness is nearly as spectacular and far more lonesome. Ask the wilderness ranger for suggestions. If he thinks you're deserving, he'll reveal a secret or two.

WASHINGTON

Washington offers some of the most varied hiking in the nation—from wilderness-ocean beaches to glaciers, from moss-carpeted rain forests to wide-sky sagebrush steppes.

People once were so few and trails so abundant the encroachment of logging roads scarcely was noticed. Now, though, loggers have chopped up so much wildland, the population has increased so greatly, and so many hikers running out of elbow room in their home states have fled to the Northwest, trails no longer are "in surplus."

The Cascade Range from the Columbia River to Snoqualmie Pass is a green sea of wooded ridges from which thrust the giant volcanoes of Mounts St. Helens, Adams, and Rainier and the volcanic roots of the Goat Rocks. Snoqualmie Pass marks the boundary of a very different geologic province, the North Cascades, and from here on the range becomes progressively broader, higher, and more sharply glacier-sculpted. The west side of the Cascades is *wet:* Late July and early August are generally fair, but even then blue skies cannot be guaranteed. Some years there is no summer at all, just a succession of cold rains between one winter and the next. The east side, the rainshadow, is kinder—frequently, while the west is being drenched, tundras of Chelan and Pasayten country are sun-bright.

A climber never can run out of challenges in Washington. Innumerable "scramble" peaks bridge the gap between trail-walking and difficult climbing. Particularly interesting

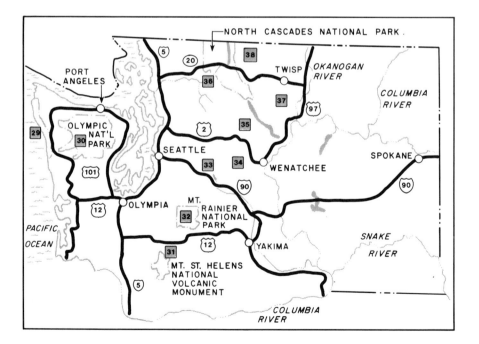

Sunrise Lake, Golden Lakes loop

Toleak Point, Olympic National Park

are the thousands of mixed routes over rock and snow and ice—truly "alpine" ascents, many short and simple, others long and complex. Containing three-fourths of the glacier area in the old 48, Washington is the ice capital of America—excluding Alaska, of course.

The longest wilderness hiking beach in the contiguous 48 states—Olympic Wilderness Beach—is found in Olympic National Park. Though hiking the full length as one continuous trip is not practical, Hike 29 tells how to do sections, as either day hikes or backpacks. Olympic National Park is also famous for moss-covered forest, rivers, lakes, glacier-clad mountains, abundant wildlife, and miles of trails, all of which can be found in the Hoh River–Glacier Basin–High Divide trip (Hike 30).

The May 1980 eruption exploded Mount St. Helens into world-wide fame. The blast changed the mountain from a symmetrically perfect ice-capped cone to a gaping crater and leveled miles of virgin forest. The Loowit and Mt. Margaret trails in the Mount St. Helens National Volcanic Monument (Hike 31) explore the moonscape of pumice fields and the toppled forest, and give close views of wildflowers that have returned.

In Mount Rainier National Park, the Wonderland Trail circles Mt. Rainier, traversing glaciers deeply creased with crevasses, crossing raging torrents on swinging bridges, dipping into virgin forest, and climbing to large alpine meadows. Hike 32 describes a day-hike sampler on the trail and the entire circuit on a two-week backpack.

The Pacific Crest National Scenic Trail (PCT) traverses mountain ridges from Mexico to Canada. In the state of Washington, the last 252 miles of the PCT north

of Snoqualmie Pass attain a spectacular climax. There is not space in this book to give the day-by-day details a hiker wants, but Hike 33 summarizes the route and outlines a day-hike sampler and week-long backpacks.

The Alpine Lakes Wilderness, a wilderness of forest, alpine meadows, and hundreds of mountain lakes, is beloved by local folks. Of the many superb trails, the one to the dozen or more lakes in the Enchantments (Hike 34) is the favorite.

Glacier Peak, its sprawling icefields flanked by alpine meadows, is the focus, yet even if this splendid volcano were absent, the Glacier Peak Wilderness would be famed for precipices, glaciers, forests, flower fields, and miles of trails. Hike 35 to Image Lake is a great among the greatest.

In North Cascades National Park, near the Canadian border, the Cascade Range rears up and sprawls out in a rugged climax of glaciers and dramatic peaks. Flower gardens are generally small, clinging to the sides of steep mountains. Trails are few. The one to Cascade Pass (Hike 36), built by miners before the turn of the century, gives easy access into the heart of this spectacular country.

In the Sawtooth Range Roadless Area, a milder climate, friendlier mountains, and miles of alpine meadows and lakes distinguish the little-used Golden Lakes trail (Hike 37), a joyous opportunity for (relative) solitude.

The Pasayten Wilderness is vast, with long valley trails climbing to alpine meadows along the Canadian border. The Cathedral Lakes trail (Hike 38) has the added attraction of lakes.

29 ▪ Olympic Wilderness Beach

DAY HIKE OR BACKPACK
Taylor Point

BACKPACK
Wilderness Beach
One way • 48 miles
Hiking time • 10 days

RESOURCES

Hikable • all year
Management • Olympic National Park
USGS maps • La Push, Forks, Cape Flattery, Ozette Lake
Hiker maps • Custom Correct North Pacific Coast, South Pacific Coast
Information • Olympic National Park, 600 E. Park Avenue, Port Angeles, Washington
  98362; phone (206) 452-4501
Permits • Backcountry permit required for overnight use
Protection status • Olympic National Park

Wide beaches, dramatic headlands, needlelike offshore islands, and wildlife of land, sea, and sky make the ocean front of Olympic National Park unique in the contiguous 48 states.

The wilderness beach of Olympic National Park extends from Shi Shi Beach south some 48 (hiking) miles to the Hoh River. The way lies mainly on the very beach, but not entirely. Certain of the jutting headlands can be rounded only at very low tides

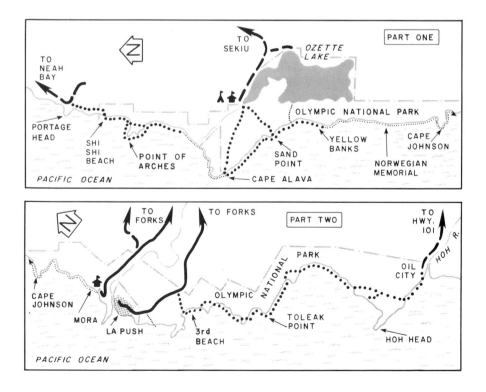

Near Rialto Beach

Graveyard of the Giants, Third Beach

and in the calmest water, and some must be crossed by trail. Portions of the way between Point of Arches and Cape Alava are blocked by cliffs: The Ozette River can be forded only during rare dry spells; a car or boat is needed to cross the Quillayute. The Olympic Wilderness Beach cannot be hiked as one continuous trip.

The absence of public transportation to the wilderness beachheads makes two cars essential for a one-way trip: Most hikers are content to do the beach in bits and pieces, hitting their favorite parts on one-, two-, or three-day round trips. Following are three representative examples, described from north to south.

Point of Arches

Round trip • 7 miles
USGS maps • Cape Flattery, Ozette Lake
Note: In 1991 the access road was temporarily closed. Check at the National Park
    Visitors Center in Port Angeles.

From Port Angeles drive SR 112 to Neah Bay on the Makah Indian Reservation. Then follow signs to "Ocean Beaches," crossing and recrossing private logging roads to the end of the public road on Portage Head. If parking service is available for a fee, use it to avoid having your car vandalized.

From the road-end walk the long-abandoned Coast Guard road south 1¹/₂ miles to the start of wide, sandy Shi Shi Beach and another 2 miles to its end at Point of Arches, which can be explored at low tide. The 6 miles beyond to Cape Alava have too many hazards to be recommended, so return to the trailhead.

Cape Alava–Sand Point Loop
Loop trip • 9$^1/_2$ miles

Cape Alava–Ruby Beach
One way • 23 miles

A forest trail to sandy beaches, the site of an historic Indian village, and fascinating Indian pictographs. Before taking this hike, visit the Makah Museum in Neah Bay to see the artifacts that were preserved when the Ozette village was buried in a gigantic mudslide some 500 years ago.

Drive SR 112, as described above, past the town of Sekiu, turn left to Ozette Lake, and park near the ranger station.

Hike 3$^1/_2$ miles through forest and bogs, the path sometimes gravel, sometimes boardwalks, to the sandy beach near Cape Alava. The loop route heads south, but don't be in a hurry. First, explore the beach north to the Ozette River. At low tide find the rusted chain, pegged oak bottom, and 3-ton anchor of the bark *Austria,* wrecked here in 1887; also study the odd rounded rocks of Cannon Ball Beach.

Southward on the beach the way rounds the minor point of "Wedding Rock." At high-tide level are dozens of fine Indian pictographs but watch carefully—they are easy to miss. Proceed along the beach to Sand Point, 3 miles from Cape Alava, and find the return trail to Ozette Lake. Before starting inland, spend another day exploring the sandy beach south 3 miles to Yellow Banks, where placer miners used to run the gold-bearing beach sand through sluice boxes. The next 12$^1/_2$ miles to the Quillayute River are mostly rocky beach.

Taylor Point
Round trip • 7 miles

Toleak Point
Round trip • 13 miles

Third Beach–Hoh River
One way • 15$^1/_2$ miles

A hiker with time for only a single stretch of beach should choose this. Drive 2 miles north of the town of Forks on US 101. Turn west 12 miles on the road toward the Indian village of La Push. Before arriving there park at Third Beach trailhead (a high-vandalism area, so leave nothing of value in the car). A good deal of the route can only be traveled in the very few hours of quite low tide, putting a day trip out of the question except for the swiftest pedestrian.

Hike 1$^1/_2$ miles in moss-covered forest to Third Beach and 1 mile south on the wide, sandy beach to the start of the trail that climbs steeply to the top of Taylor Point. Day-hikers do well to turn back here. The 1-mile trail climbs the point and then plummets down the far side to the beach near Scotts Bluff, which can be rounded when the tide is low enough or otherwise crossed via a short up–down path. Scott Creek is a problem in high water but usually crossable on driftwood. Several small points are rounded before Toleak Point, 6$^1/_2$ miles. Plan to camp hereabouts and spend a day exploring part of the remaining 9 miles to Hoh River, much of the way on forest trail with spectacular views and delightful waterfalls.

30 • Hoh Rain Forest

DAY HIKE
Happy Four Camp
Round trip • 11½ miles
Hiking time • 6 hours
High point • 800 feet
Elevation gain • 225 feet
Hikable • all year

BACKPACK
Blue Glacier and High Divide
Round trip • 47 miles (to Blue Glacier 37 miles)
Hiking time • 6 days
High point • 5474 feet
Elevation gain • 8100 feet (to Blue Glacier 3700 feet)
Hikable • mid-July through September

RESOURCES
Management • Olympic National Park
USGS maps • Bogachiel Peak, Mt. Carrie, Mount Tom
Hiker map • Custom Correct Mount Olympus
Information • Olympic National Park, 600 E. Park Avenue, Port Angeles, Washington 98362; phone (206) 452-4501
Permits • Backcountry permit required for overnight use
Protection status • Olympic National Park

A long valley approach through a magnificent rain forest to alpine flower fields and a choice of touching the edge of the Blue Glacier on Mt. Olympus or attaining the famous High Divide view over the green depths of the Hoh River to the Alaskalike icefields beyond. Alpine lakes and good chances of seeing elk, deer, and bear give this trip an almost perfect rating.

Drive 12 miles south of Forks on US 101. Turn east 19 miles on the Hoh River road to the road-end and trailhead at the Rain Forest Visitor Center, elevation 578 feet.

Find the Hoh River trail in the maze of superb nature trails near the visitor center and head upriver in the world-renowned rain forest of gigantic hemlocks, cedar, spruce,

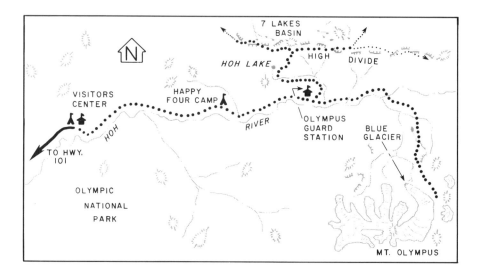

and fir, moss-draped maples, and a thickly moss-covered forest floor. The valley is home year-round to a band of elk, often seen near the trail in early morning and the evidence of their residence—huge hoof prints, grazed and trampled vegetation, and droppings—seen everywhere. At 5$^1/_2$ miles is Happy Four Camp, a good destination for a day hike.

The trail continues past Lewis Meadow, the site of a pioneer ranch, still 8 miles from the nearest road and many more than that when it was inhabited, and at 9 miles the Olympus Guard Station. At 9$^1/_2$ miles the trail splits, forcing the difficult decision between the Blue Glacier and the High Divide. Do both. First, the glacier. Continue up the Hoh River trail, crossing the river at 12 miles and climbing out of the valley to Elk Lake at 15 miles. The way steepens and views open at Glacier Meadows, 17$^1/_2$ miles. Follow the climbers' path to the moraine at the edge of the Blue Glacier and its hard, blue ice creased with deep crevasses. Do not venture onto the surface unless properly trained and equipped.

Having returned to the junction near Olympus Guard Station, ascend 3500 feet in 5 miles out of forest to meadows and Hoh Lake. Another 1$^1/_2$ miles of flower gardens lead to 5474-foot Bogachiel Peak, a former lookout site on High Divide offering climax views. High Divide can be reached by a shorter trail from Sol Duc Hot Springs, so don't expect to be lonesome.

Hoh Rain Forest

Mount St. Helens from Norway Pass

31 ▪ Mount Margaret–Loowit Trail

DAY HIKE	BACKPACK
Mount Margaret	**Loowit Trail**
Round trip • 11 miles	Loop trip • 31 miles
Hiking time • 6 hours	Hiking time • 3 days
High point • 5858 feet	High point • 4800 feet
Elevation gain • 2300 feet	Elevation gain • 4100 feet

RESOURCES

Hikable • late July through September
Management • Mount St. Helens National Volcanic Monument, Gifford Pinchot
    National Forest
USGS map • Spirit Lake
Hiker map • None
Information • Mount St. Helens National Volcanic Monument, Amboy, Washington
    98601; phone (206) 247-5473
Protection status • Mount St. Helens National Volcanic Monument

The May 1980 eruption of Mount St. Helens that so drastically reshaped the landscape also disrupted an extensive trail system. New trails have been built and are becoming as famous as any in the nation. The best day hike to appreciate the force of the initial blast and the remains of the mountain that was once called the Mt. Fuji of the West is a day hike to Mt. Margaret by way of Norway Pass. The backpack is the Loowit Trail circling the volcano. (Loowit was the lovely maiden who long, long ago was turned into, what was until 1980, a lovely mountain.) While the loop is less than 25 miles, the trail does not touch a road, so the access trail is added to the total

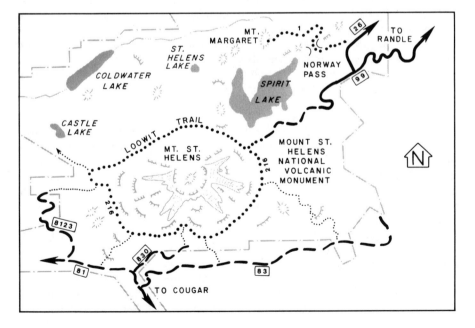

Loowit Trail crossing pumice slope

distance. The trail is not easy, dropping into deep gullies and crossing fields of lava blocks and pumice slopes as tiring as soft snow; many miles are wide-open to sun, wind, and dust storms of volcanic ash. However, there is no better way to fully appreciate the cataclysm of May 18, 1980. There are seven possible starting points. The trail is described here (but not necessarily recommended) starting at Windy Point.

From the town of either Cougar on the south or Randle on the north, drive road No. 25 and turn uphill on No. 99, signed "Windy Pass," to a junction at 9 miles. For the day hike to Mt. Margaret, go right 1 mile on No. 26 to the Norway Pass trailhead, elevation 3600 feet.

The Norway Pass–Mt. Margaret trail plunges into the blast area. Though toppled trees are seen beside the road, a deeper feeling for the event is gained while switchbacking up the bleakly deforested hillside. Note the small trees that survived by being seedlings, deeply buried in springtime snow. Note how the fallen trees on slopes facing Mount St. Helens are neatly laid out parallel to one another, pointing away from the mountain, while on the slopes facing away from the mountain they are piled like jackstraws from eddies of the blast.

At 2 miles are Norway Pass and a view of Mount St. Helens and Spirit Lake. Note the driftwood covering the lake and the hillsides that were swept clean for a good 500 feet above the shore by the tremendous *seiche* ("tidal wave").

From the pass the trail climbs slopes of Mt. Margaret into alpine flower fields that were protected by the snow, which still lay 4–5 feet deep at the time of the eruption. At 5 1/2 miles the trail tops the central peak of 5858-foot Mt. Margaret, offering views of other giant volcanoes of the Cascade Range. Study them with a new suspicion. Ponder what it would have been like to have been here on that horrendous day. The trail continues on, crossing the monument from east to west in about 15 miles. Camping along the way is pretty grim and the water questionable.

For the Loowit Trail backpack, follow the day-hike driving instructions to the junction on road No. 99 and continue on No. 99 to the road-end at Windy Pass, elevation 4000 feet. Walk the gated service road signed "Truman Trail No. 207" toward the mountain for 2 miles, first climbing a bit, and then going down to a dry wash. Leave the road here and go up the dry wash 1 mile on the obscure Windy Trail No. 216E (more of a route than a trail), at one place scrambling, to intersect Loowit Trail No. 216 at 4500 feet. Please note: Stay with the wash or existing trail; the barren pumice slopes are easily disrupted by feet. (To protect the sensitive environment, hikers are prohibited from wandering more than 10 feet from the trail anywhere in the Spirit Lake Basin.)

Once on the Loowit Trail, head west on slopes of pumice, traversing between Spirit Lake and the gaping crater, with views of miles and miles of barren hills that were denuded by the blast, whose force extended 14–17 miles to the west. At approximately 7 miles reach Castle Ridge and at 4000 feet join a section of Toutle trail No. 238. Keep left, dropping steeply into the loose ash of the Pumice Bowl, to a crossing of South Fork Toutle River. A bit farther is an intersection, at about 2800 feet. For an excellent campsite follow the Toutle trail a scant ¹/₂ mile to a stream.

To continue the loop, the Loowit Trail climbs out of the blast area, partly in virgin forest, partly in scorched trees and flower fields, to a 4700-foot high point on Crescent Ridge. The trail descends into an alpine forest. With many ups and downs the way climbs again to timberline and at approximately 5¹/₂ miles from the South Fork Toutle reaches a junction with Butte Camp trail No. 238A. Find campsites with water at Butte Camp, a 1¹/₄-mile detour and 800-foot elevation loss.

In the next 5 miles the tread becomes rougher and routefinding tricky, the trail often obscure as it crosses lava fields, losing 1400 feet to a junction with the June Lake trail; there are campsites at June Lake, a ¹/₃-mile sidetrip. The next 4³/₄ miles are equally difficult, traversing more cruel lava flows to a junction with the Ape Canyon trail. The next 4 miles are easier as the trail crosses the Plains of Abraham to the final junction. Turn right and return 2 miles to the Windy Point parking lot.

Spreading phlox

Mount Rainier and field of avalanche lilies in Spray Park

32 ▪ Wonderland Trail

DAY HIKE
Indian Henry's Hunting Ground
Round trip • 7 miles
Hiking time • 4 hours
High point • 5400 feet
Elevation gain • 2200 feet

BACKPACK
Wonderland Trail
Loop trip • 93 miles
Hiking time • 14 days
High point • 6750 feet
Elevation gain • 20,000 feet

RESOURCES
Hikable • mid-July through September
Management • Mount Rainier National Park
USGS maps • Mount Rainier National Park or Mt. Rainier West, Mt. Wow, Golden
  Lakes, Mowich Lake, Sunrise, Chinook Pass, Mt. Rainier East
Hiker maps • Green Trails Mt. Rainier–West and Mt. Rainier–East
Information • Mount Rainier National Park, Tahoma Woods, Star Route, Ashford,
  Washington 98304; phone (206) 569-2211
Permits • Backcountry permit required for overnight use
Protection status • Mount Rainier National Park

The trail that completely circles Mt. Rainier is often called the Northwest's greatest of hikes. It climbs from valley forests to alpine meadows, skirts fields of living ice, crosses crystal streams of snowmelt and muddy torrents from the snouts of glaciers. The whole route can be done in ten days; the prudent person, however, will allow two or more weeks in order to sample the many inviting sidetrips or just soak in views and smell the flowers.

Unfortunately, the backpack doesn't rate five stars from a backpacker because the Park Service, in order to give a higher quality of wilderness experience to fewer people, has drastically limited the number and capacity of campsites. The result is trails crowded with day-hikers and severely restricted options for backpackers.

The Wonderland Trail can be day-hiked and sampled from a dozen or more starting points around the mountain. A favorite is Indian Henry's Hunting Ground, a 7-mile round trip that gains 2200 feet and is reached from the Nisqually Entrance and the West Side Road near the Nisqually Entrance. Be sure to add the 3/4-mile sidetrip to tiny Mirror Lake and its acres of wildflowers.

Note: The recommended route for the day hike to Indian Henry's Hunting Ground may be blocked by reoccurring flash floods that some years have forced closure of the access road. If so, start the day on the Kautz Creek trail, adding 4 miles to the round trip.

The Wonderland Trail can be started from any of the park's roads and hiked in either direction. Because of bus access, it is described here from Longmire, reached from SR 706 on the south side of the mountain, elevation 2750 feet.

Camping permits for the Wonderland Trail can best be obtained at the Longmire Visitors Center. The rangers do their best to help hikers plan their trip and match the

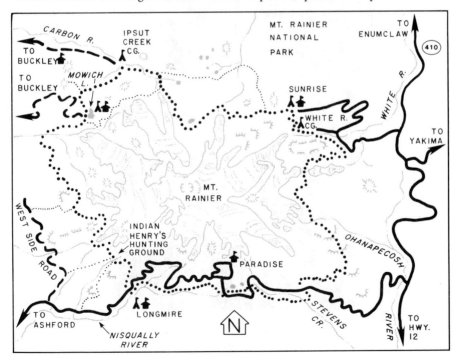

campsites to the hikers' ability. If, for whatever reason, the campsite schedule cannot be maintained, backcountry rangers will devise a substitute itinerary.

The Wonderland Trail leaves the visitors center, in ¹/₄ mile crosses the Paradise Highway, ascends Rampart Ridge, drops to Kautz Creek, and climbs to the flower fields of Indian Henry's Hunting Ground, 5400 feet. The way thence is down to a swaying suspension bridge across the deep canyon of Tahoma Creek, over the crest of 5600-foot Emerald Ridge, and down beside the Tahoma Glacier to the South Puyallup River bridge. The next stage is through Sunset Park past Golden Lakes, down from meadowland to a crossing of the Mowich River, and up to a road-end campground at Mowich Lake, 32¹/₂ miles from Longmire.

The up-and-down way proceeds over Ipsut Pass to a suspension bridge across the Carbon River, a long climb above the Carbon Glacier to 6004-foot Moraine Park, down to Mystic Lake and Winthrop Creek, over 6700-foot Skyscraper Pass, past Sunrise Visitors Center and snack bar, and down to the White River Campground, 30¹/₂ miles from Mowich Lake.

The final stage climbs from the White River to flower fields of Summerland, traverses the naked slopes and summer snowfields of Panhandle Gap, 6700 feet, and descends to more flower fields at Indian Bar. The way drops into forest, crosses Stevens Canyon Highway to Maple Creek, on a final ascent crosses the highway twice again, and passes the last alpine meadow at Reflection Lake before descending into the Nisqually Valley and returning to Longmire, 31 miles from the White River.

Above: *Avalanche lilies.* Opposite: *Klapatche Park and Mount Rainier*

33 ▪ Pacific Crest National Scenic Trail –Snoqualmie Pass North

DAY HIKE
Kendall Katwalk
Round trip • 10 miles
Hiking time • 5 hours
High point • 5400 feet
Elevation gain • 2700 feet in, 300 feet out

BACKPACK
Pacific Crest National Scenic Trail
One way • Snoqualmie Pass to Canada
  252 miles
Hiking time • 30 days
High point • 6900 feet
Elevation gain • 40,000 feet

RESOURCES

Hikable • mid-July to October
Management • Mount Baker–Snoqualmie, Wenatchee, and Okanogan National Forests
USGS maps • Snoqualmie Pass and about 10 others
Hiker map • Forest Service Pacific Crest National Scenic Trail–Washington State Northern Portion
Information • Forest Service/National Park Service Outdoor Recreation Information Center, Federal Building, 915 2nd Avenue, Seattle, Washington 98104; phone (206) 553-0170
Protection status • Pacific Crest National Scenic Trail

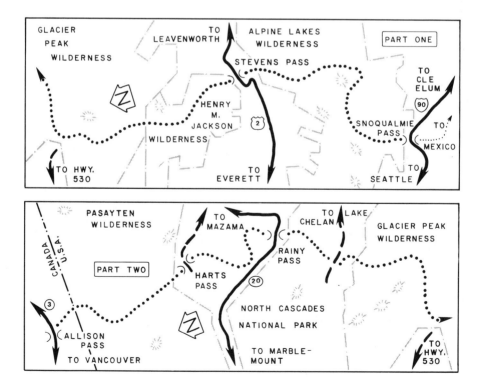

North of Snoqualmie Pass the Pacific Crest National Scenic Trail (PCT) is not marred by depressing stretches of clearcuts as it is to the south—most of the way to Canada lies within protected wilderness. Lakes are numerous. Deer, bear, elk, and mountain goats are frequently seen. Valley forests are ancient and highland scenery magnificent. Definitely a great hike. No section can be recommended above others. They're all great. A month or more is needed to do the entire 252 miles in a single go and that entails complex logistics of food resupply. The popular itinerary, therefore, is three or four trips of about ten days each. More common than that is sampling the route on hikes of one or two days.

Vehicle access for starting and ending (and resupply) are I-90 at Snoqualmie Pass, US 2 at Stevens Pass, North Cascades Highway at Rainy Pass, forest road No. 54 at Harts Pass, and Canada Highway 3 at Allison Pass.

No book of great hikes would be complete without the PCT. Unfortunately, because of space limitation, the following description is sketchy. While the Forest Service map gives excellent travel directions, to properly describe the experience of the PCT demands a whole book. We recommend the Wilderness Press volume *Pacific Crest Trail Volume 2: Oregon and Washington.*

Mountain goats on Pacific Crest National Scenic Trail near Cutthroat Pass

Pacific Crest National Scenic Trail near Benson Pass

Snoqualmie Pass to Stevens Pass

One way • 67 miles
Hiking time • 6 days
High point • 5800 feet

Elevation gain • 10,600 feet
Hikable • mid-July to early October

Thanks to regularly scheduled buses over both passes, the 67 miles can be done as a one-way hike with no private automobiles involved. Travelers from across America arrive in Seattle by bus, train, or air and employ public transportation to and from the trailheads.

The trail quickly climbs from forest at Snoqualmie Pass to flowers and panoramas on Kendall Peak, making this far and away the best easy sampler. However, here is also the greatest potential for extreme danger on the PCT, the Kendall Katwalk, a narrow ledge blasted from a granite cliff. Snowbanks may linger far into summer and on any summer day a sudden snowstorm may blow in; the ledge is then perilous for any but a trained climber.

The route is nearly entirely in the Alpine Lakes Wilderness, passing numerous lakes, alternating between high meadows and virgin forests.

Stevens Pass to Rainy Pass

One way • 114 miles
Hiking time • 15 days
High point • 6438 feet

Elevation gain • 17,000 feet
Hikable • mid-July to early October

The longest and most varied section of the PCT climbs from valley-bottom forest to miles of meadows brilliant with flowers, drops to forest, climbs again, over and over. The way rounds the slopes of Glacier Peak and is steadily in close view of other ice-covered mountains. The route is mainly in the Glacier Peak Wilderness; short bits are in the Henry M. Jackson Wilderness and North Cascades National Park.

Rainy Pass to Harts Pass

One way • 31 miles
Hiking time • 4 days
High point • 6700 feet

Elevation gain • 4400 feet
Hikable • late July to early October

Steep ridges of meadows and cliffs, endless vistas of snowcapped mountains, as scenically grand as any other part of the trail, yet—due to legislative oversight—the one stretch not yet having wilderness protection. The terrain is such that roads are no threat and the forests are of an alpine sort that rules out logging. However, the possibility exists of commercial helicopter service bringing in tourists for an hour of sightseeing. "Roadless" no longer necessarily means "wild."

Harts Pass to Allison Pass

One way • 40 miles
Hiking time • 5 days
High point • 6900 feet

Elevation gain • 8000 feet
Hikable • late July through September

The final leg of the route to Canada is almost constantly above timberline in broad expanses of flowery meadows. Snow lasts late and comes early in these highlands of the Pasayten Wilderness; when it's springtime in the Sierra at 2 miles high it's still winter here at 1 mile.

Pika drying leaves

Prusik Peak and Gnome Tarn

34 · Enchantment Lakes

DAY HIKE
None

BACKPACK
Enchantment Lakes
Round trip • 20 miles
Hiking time • 3–4 days
High point • 7000 feet
Elevation gain • 5400 feet

RESOURCES

Hikable • late July to mid-October
Management • Wenatchee National Forest
USGS map • Enchantment Lakes
Hiker map • Wenatchee National Forest Recreation Map
Information • Leavenworth Ranger District, 600 Sherbourne, Leavenworth,
   Washington 98826; phone (509) 548-5817
Permits • Enchantment Lakes permits required; write or phone the Leavenworth
   Ranger Station
Protection status • Alpine Lakes Wilderness

Start with the negative: The elevation gain is formidable to a person burdened by
a heavy stone on his back. The altitude is so high that many a summer never comes—
the old snows of the past winter are barely half-melted before the new snows of the
coming winter are falling. Fame has brought such heavy traffic that the Forest Service
first had to curtail horses, then dogs and campfires, and, finally, to preserve the quality
of the environment and the experience, limit visitation to 100 people per day; reservations
must be made well in advance.

For all that, a list of great hikes that omitted the Enchantments would be a
laughingstock. To be sure, the Alpine Lakes Wilderness has many other glories, including
the "Mormon Lakes" area of Ladies Pass, across the Icicle valley from the Enchantments,
also crowded. There are "secret spots," too, perhaps a tad less spectacular, compensating
with solitude. But at least once in a lifetime a hiker must go on a pilgrimage to the
Enchantments. The granite spires and cliffs of the "Cashmere Crags," the granite slabs
plucked and polished and scratched by the glaciers, closely resemble the truly high (above
12,000 feet) High Sierra. One difference is that the air is more breathable at 7000 feet.
Another is that the glaciers are not a remote geologic memory, as in most of the Sierra;
when the lakes were discovered, early in this century, there weren't as many as now—
because the entire upper basin was still under ice. Finally, in addition to heather and
huckleberries, flowers and waterfalls (and lakes), there is the Lyall larch. Photographers
flock here in late September to capture the low autumn sun igniting golden torches.

Drive US 2 to Leavenworth. Pick up permits at the Forest Service station on the

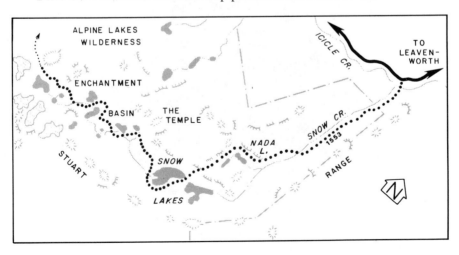

east edge of town. At the west edge of town turn south 4 miles on Icicle River Road to the Snow Lakes parking lot, elevation 1600 feet.

Snow Lakes Trail No. 1553 crosses Icicle Creek on a sturdy bridge and sets out switchbacking, relentlessly gaining 3400 feet in $5^1/_2$ miles to Nada Lake, 5000 feet. To break up the labor, some parties start in the cool of late afternoon and camp the first night partway up the creek. The ascent continues to Snow Lakes, 5415 feet, $6^3/_4$ miles. Above there the trail emerges from deep forest as it climbs 1500 feet in another 3 miles through meadows and cliffs to the Lower Enchantments, entering the basin near Lake Vivianne, 7000 feet.

We designate this the turnaround point for the three- to four-day backpack. Most parties find a schedule of one and one-half days to Snow Lakes, a day to explore to Vivianne, and a day out is strenuous enough. But of course, spectacular as Vivianne is in its granite bowl beneath Merlin's Tower, the granite blade of Excalibur thrusting out in the blue waters, this is only the beginning. For that once-in-a-lifetime experience, a hiker really needs a full week.

Follow the stream upward through the Lower Basin, passing one lake after another and tiny tarns between. A steep granite step leads to a whole other world, the basin of the Upper Enchantments, a half-century ago all glacier, now lakes and moraines and tarns and snowfields (and ice scraps) rising to Aasgard Pass, 7750 feet, beneath the cliffs of Dragontail Peak, a moderate one-day round trip from Vivianne. Be warned: A party that comes this far in early October for the goldening of the larch must be prepared to flee a sudden fury of whitening.

Above: *Rocky campsite near Lake Viviane*
Opposite: *Leprechaun Lake*

35 ▪ Image Lake

DAY HIKE	BACKPACK
None	**Image Lake**
	Round trip • 32 miles
	Hiking time • 3–4 days
	High point • 6100 feet
	Elevation gain • 4500 feet

RESOURCES

Hikable • mid-July to late September
Management • Mount Baker–Snoqualmie National Forest
USGS maps • Glacier Peak, Holden
Hiker map • USFS Glacier Peak Wilderness
Information • Darrington Ranger District, Darrington, Washington 98241; phone
    (206) 436-1155
Protection status • Glacier Peak Wilderness

A strenuous hike to one of the most famous mountain panoramas in the country. What with wildflowers, wild water, and wild forests added in, the trip satisfies four of the six criteria for greatness. As for the last two, animals are scarce because people definitely are not.

From a car window a person can see and photograph the other views so common on calendars and travel brochures—Mt. Rainier, Crater Lake, the Grand Tetons, Mount St. Helens, and Grand Canyon. Of the "top ten" in the calendar poll, only Glacier Peak and its reflection in Image Lake demand muscle power.

From SR 530 near the crossing of the Sauk River, turn onto Suiattle River road No. 26 and drive 23 miles to its end and the trailhead, elevation 1600 feet.

Trail No. 784 follows the Suiattle River 9½ miles to a junction. Go left on Miners Ridge trail No. 785 and begin interminable switchbacks. At 13 miles stay left again, climbing to meadow country, Glacier Peak tall and huge across the deep, wide valley.

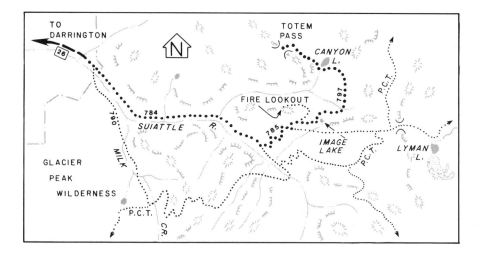

Image Lake and Glacier Peak

At about 15 miles pass a sidetrail to Miners Ridge Lookout. At 16 miles reach the famous view at Image Lake, 6100 feet. Campsites are located below the outlet; the outdoor privy there must have the country's greatest view.

Having come this far, spend two to three days exploring. Visit the Miners Ridge fire lookout. Go east along the ridge through flower gardens to the horse camp at Ladies Camp. Follow a deadend trail northward past Canyon Lake to Totem Pass and the flowers of the Hanging Gardens. While the scenery isn't (can't get) any better, one can extend the time spent by backpacking another 12 miles to the snout of the Lyman Glacier or return high on the slopes of Glacier Peak by way of the Milk Creek–Dolly Creek trail.

36 • Cascade Pass

DAY HIKE
Cascade Pass–Sahale Arm
Round trip • 11 miles
Hiking time • 10 hours
High point • 7600 feet
Elevation gain • 4000 feet

BACKPACK
Cascade Pass–Park Creek Pass
One way • 33 miles
Hiking time • 5 days
High point • 6100 feet
Elevation gain • 5700 feet

RESOURCES

Hikable • mid-July to October
Management • North Cascades National Park
USGS maps • Cascade Pass, Forbidden Peak, Goode Mtn., Mt. Logan, Diablo Dam
Hiker maps • Green Trails Cascade Pass, McGregor Mtn., Mt. Logan, Diablo
Information • North Cascades National Park, 2105 Highway 20, Sedro Woolley,
    Washington 98284; phone (206) 856-5700
Permits • Backcountry permit required for overnight camping
Protection status • North Cascades National Park

The North Cascades Highway is touted as the most scenic drive in the state; the touting is done by folks who don't know the state very well. To be sure, it has its moments. But they are mighty tame stuff compared to the short and easy trail to Cascade Pass. The awesome scenery is enough to earn a great rating. Across the deep valley a half-dozen glaciers send avalanches crashing down mile-high cliffs. From the flower meadow of the pass are views over range upon range of glaciered mountains. The day hike, among the most spectacular samplers of the North Cascades, is recommended; the backpack requires a second car parked at the Colonial Creek Campground.

Drive to the town of Marblemount on the North Cascades Highway, SR 20. For

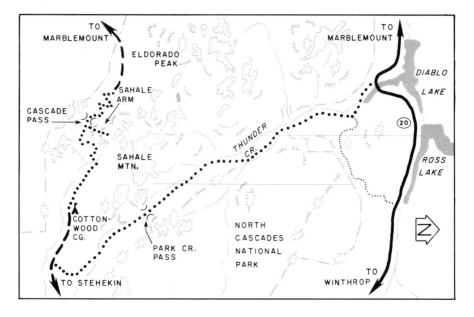

the traverse continue past Newhalem to Colonial Creek Campground. Leave a car and return to Marblemount. For the start of both the day hike to Cascade Pass and the traverse, at Marblemount cross the Skagit River and follow the Cascade River road 25 miles to the road-end and trailhead, elevation 3600 feet. The parking lot itself has more stunning views of avalanches and hanging glaciers than any on the North Cascades Highway; the trail adds drama with every step.

Fortunately, the trail is wide enough to accommodate the hundreds who on every fair Sunday walk the 3^1/$_2$ miles to the pass. Experienced hikers are frustrated by the endless switchbacks but the majority of visitors never have been on a real mountain trail before and consider the way steep. However, even at the slowest of paces, the way eventually climbs above timberline to alpine meadows with breathtaking views that culminate at Cascade Pass, 5400 feet. On peak-use days a park ranger is on hand, happy to point out landmarks.

The pass is plenty far enough for most folks and quite an accomplishment for a novice. However, even grander sights await above. A steeper but well-defined path climbs

Magic Mountain from Sahale Arm

from the north side of the pass. The higher it goes along the meadow crest of Sahale Arm the broader the horizons, until finally the way ends on the terminal moraine of the little Sahale Glacier, whose hidden crevasses put it off-limits to hikers. The views from here of ice-chiseled peaks and peak-chiseling glaciers are the most extensive and impressive of any trail in the West.

Views are no better (they couldn't be!) on the backpack but there are more of them. And more ancient forests. From Cascade Pass descend eastward into the Stehekin Valley, at 5 miles from Cascade Pass hitting the road-end at Cottonwood Camp. Ride the shuttle bus 5 miles to the Park Creek Pass trailhead and resume walking. The trail climbs 3700 feet in 8 miles to the 6100-foot pass. It then descends from alpine meadows to magnificent forests of Thunder Creek, at 18 miles from the pass reaching Diablo Lake Campground on the North Cascades Highway.

37 • Crater Lake–Golden Lakes Loop

DAY HIKE
Crater Lake
Round trip • 8 miles
Hiking time • 5 hours
High point • 6841 feet
Elevation gain • 2100 feet

BACKPACK
Golden Lakes Loop
Loop trip • 23 miles
Hiking time • 3 days
High point • 8000 feet
Elevation gain • 5500 feet

RESOURCES

Hikable • mid-July to October
Management • Okanogan National Forest
USGS map • Martin Peak
Hiker map • Green Trails Prince Creek
Information • Twisp Ranger District, Twisp, Washington 98856; phone (509) 997-2131
Protection status • Unprotected

The groves of mountain hemlock and subalpine fir dotting the meadows are green year-round. In fall, however, the Lyall larch, the evergreen that is not, turns golden. Golden, too, in that season are the meadows that sweep from cliffs and snowfields down to shores of the five lakes sparkling in old glacier cirques.

The rainshadow (east) side of the North Cascades has many a scene equally praiseworthy. The reason we chose the Golden Lakes for our collection of greats is the solitude. When nearby national parks and national wildernesses are busy with boots, the trails here are lonesome. Finding a private—and great—campsite is easy.

Of all the hikes in this book, this comes the closest to encompassing all six components of a great hike. The credit for the solitude goes—paradoxically—to motorcycles. The country properly belongs in the Chelan–Sawtooth Wilderness, but Okanogan National Forest has instead dedicated it to multiple-recreation, meaning machines. The irony is that motorcyclists are less interested in scenery and lakes than maneuvering wheels through obstacle courses; they rarely ride this trail, which would give them only an hour or two of amusement, not worth the long drive to the trailhead. On the other hand, hikers

Cooney Lake

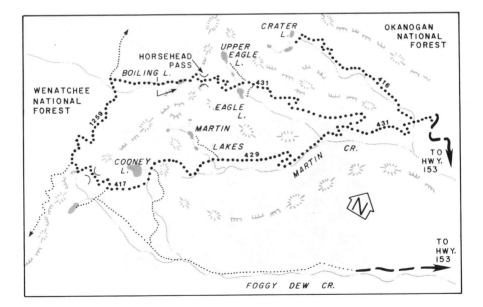

so hate motorcycles they avoid the trail as if it were infected with the plague. Granted, during three days on the loop a hiker may meet one or several machines, and that's bad. But not bad enough to mar the miles and hours of never seeing or hearing another human, on foot or horse or wheel.

From Pateros on the Columbia River drive 17 miles on SR 153. Turn left on a narrow county road signed "Gold Creek," then left again on forest road No. 4340. At 6.6 miles from the highway keep straight on road No. (4340)300 a final 6 miles to Eagle Lakes Trail No. 431, elevation 4700 feet.

Because one of the many junctions is hard to find when doing the loop counterclockwise, the clockwise direction is recommended. Follow the Eagle Lakes Trail a scant mile to a junction. For the day hike (or an easier backback) take the motorfree right fork climbing in 3 miles to Crater Lake, surrounded by trees, flowers, and peaks.

For the backpack, go straight ahead. At 2 miles from the road turn left on Martin Creek trail No. 429. Drop to a crossing of Eagle Creek and commence a series of long switchbacks up through forest. At 6½ miles from the road pass a sidetrail that climbs a very steep ½ mile to the two Martin Lakes, 6800 feet. The Martin Creek trail drops a bit and climbs to Cooney Lake, 7241 feet, 9 miles from the road. In summer, before the season of gold, the larches are an ethereal green. The meadows then are bright with flowers. Snowfields on the ringing peaks make waterfall music. A party may well wish to spend an extra day here, looking and listening.

Trail No. 417 (unsigned) rounds the left (south) shore and climbs to an 8000-foot pass overlooking Merchant Basin. For a great sidetrip adding another day, follow the trail down into Merchant Basin, and then climb to the shore of Sunrise Lake. For the loop, some 300 feet east of the pass is an unmarked junction. Take the right fork, contouring westward ½ mile to a second 8000-foot pass overlooking Prince Creek and Lake Chelan and descending to an unmarked junction with Chelan Summit Trail No. 420. Turn right through meadows 2½ miles to a junction with trail No. 431.

This junction is only 1½ miles from the boundary of Chelan–Sawtooth Wilderness, a glory of flower fields and lakes and easy-roaming, big-view ridges. The highlands on this dry side of the range are so open, and the sheep-grazing of years past has left so extensive a system of trails, exploration can fill a month, a summer, many summers. However, to complete our three-day loop backpack, turn right on trail No. 431, ascend past Boiling Lake to Horsehead Pass, 7590 feet, and descend (passing a ½-mile sidetrail to Upper Eagle Lake, 7110 feet) to the starting point.

Mountain daisy

38 ▪ Windy Pass–Cathedral Lakes

DAY HIKE	BACKPACK
Harts Pass–Windy Pass	**Cathedral Lakes**
Round trip • 7 miles	Round trip • 38 miles
Hiking time • 4 hours	Hiking time • 5 days
High point • 6900 feet	High point • 7600 feet
Elevation gain • 500 feet	Elevation gain • 2200 feet

RESOURCES

Hikable • July through September
Management • Okanogan National Forest
USGS maps • Coleman Peak, Bauerman Ridge, Remmel Mtn.
Hiker map • USFS Pasayten Wilderness
Information • Winthrop Ranger District, Winthrop, Washington 98865; phone (509) 996-2266
Protection status • Pasayten Wilderness

Vast expanses of flower-covered alpine meadows are common throughout the Pasayten Wilderness along the Canadian border. The easiest short sampler is from Harts Pass north on the Pacific Crest National Scenic Trail (PCT). A week or more is required to attain the heart of the wilderness, becoming totally immersed in perfume and color by the days and days and miles and miles of wildflowers. Unlike others that have just as many flowers, this hike has the superb cirque-set Cathedral Lakes and fine forests, together making the trip one of the greats.

For the sampler hike to Windy Pass, drive SR 20 west to the hamlet of Mazama, and then take the forest road up the Methow Valley to Harts Pass. Continue upward on the Slate Peak road. Find the trailhead at the first switchback and hike the PCT north 3½ miles, through acres and acres of flowers, and miles of views.

For the backpack, from Winthrop in the Methow Valley drive the Chewack River road some 30 miles to its end at 30-Mile Camp, elevation 3500 feet.

Follow the Chewack River trail No. 510 upstream 8 miles to the junction of the

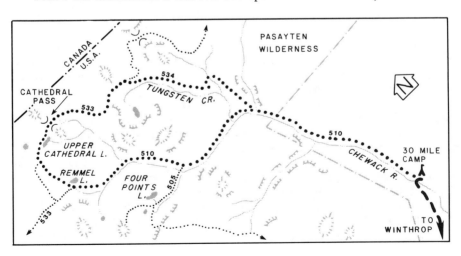

Remmel Lake

Tungsten Creek trail No. 534, the return route. At 10 miles a 3-mile sidetrip is recommended to Four Points Lake trail No. 505 and grand views on an abandoned lookout trail to the top of 8685-foot Remmel Mountain. At 12 miles, having gained only 1100 feet, the river trail finally starts upward, gently climbing 1300 feet in the next 5 miles to Remmel Lake at 17 miles, 6871 feet. The shores are ringed by picturesque trees and alpine meadows. Unfortunately, they are also usually ringed by horses and as often as not by cows. All trails in the vicinity are badly beaten up by horses. Few camps are free of apples (horse) and pies (cow).

Circle the lake and near the outlet go right, climbing to some of the largest tundras in the Cascades. In about 1 mile go left on Boundary Trail No. 533 another mile to Upper Cathedral Lake, 7400 feet, 19 miles from the trailhead.

For variety on the return trip, continue east on the Boundary Trail over 7600-foot Cathedral Pass. At 6 miles from the lake turn right on Tungsten Creek trail No. 534 and descend 5 miles to the Chewack River trail, 8 miles from the road-end.

British Columbia

By Canadian standards the lower United States has hardly any true wilderness, few real mountains, and mere snippets of ice. British Columbia is nearly as large as Washington, Oregon, Idaho, and Montana combined and half of its 2,000,000 people live in and around the single city of Vancouver, meaning there is an awful lot of empty country. These are principally *northern* ranges with enormous glaciers, brief summers, and weather varying from poor to impossible. A good share of the continent's grandest peaks are in British Columbia and adjacent Alberta, many offering ice and rock challenges to test the most daring alpinist, some accessible to none but the expedition mountaineer. Hiking opportunities, though magnificent, are restricted by the rarity of maintained trails; except in some of the national and provincial parks, hikers are not pampered the way they are south of the border. The B.C. Forest Service has been slow to accept trails as a resource and a responsibility.

The conservation ethic is barely beginning to prick the consciousness of government officials. Huge regions of matchless natural glories lack any protection at all and "belong" absolutely to loggers and miners—and dammers, who for the sake of electricity have perpetrated some of the most destructive floods since the one that made Noah a sailor. Park status means less in Canada than in the United States; considerable commercial

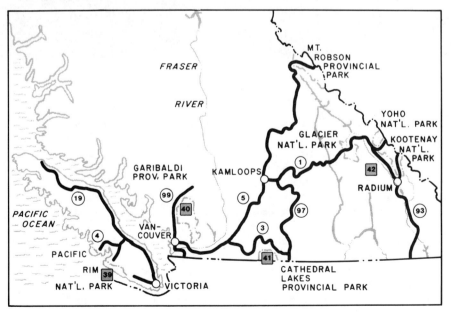

Lake of the Hanging Glacier and Commander Range

exploitation is allowed and the boundaries are subject to casual revision. Wildernesses guaranteed by statute are few and "nature conservancies" protected by administrative regulation scarce. Recreationists are doing their share to dilute the wildness—havens that would demand many strenuous days to attain on foot are cheapened by quicky-vacationers using floatplane and helicopter to plop down at the very poles of remoteness. People who at the dinner table pass up the soup, salad, meat, potatoes, and vegetables to eat only apple pie also are happy to let a chopper flop them down in a meadow or on a glacier. By not making a respectful entrance, hiking through forest, along rivers, and ever-expanding views, they do not gain a genuine wilderness experience. Worse, they ruin the experience for travelers of good taste who do the long approach through the whole wilderness and at the end of many days find the picnickers, minutes from a city, sitting in the flowers eating potato chips, drinking beer, and listening to rock and rap on portable radios.

Due to lack of maintained trails, only four great hikes are recommended.

The West Coast Trail (Hike 39) of Pacific Rim National Park is North America's longest ocean beach trail unbroken by roads. Headlands difficult to cross and bays requiring ferry service add to the remoteness and beauty that have made this trail world famous.

Garibaldi Provincial Park is the most popular hiking area in the Vancouver region. The Garibaldi Lake trail (Hike 40) switchbacks through magnificent trees to the turquoise lake and to green meadows, a cinder plateau, a lava flow, views of snowy peaks, icefields, and glaciers that descend almost to the lakeshore.

The lakes, the easy access to alpine meadows, and the views from rocky summits give Cathedral Provincial Park, on the international border, three of the six qualities of a great hike. From a basecamp at timberline, Hike 41 takes parties of small children, their parents, and their grandparents to explore the five major subalpine Cathedral Lakes and to ascend one of several trails to unmatched views of the North Cascades from the Glacier Peak Wilderness to Manning Provincial Park. The beauty of the country is especially intense in October when the larch trees around the high lakes turn a glowing yellow-orange.

In the stampede to the world-famous, always crowded trails in the Canadian Rockies, most hikers ignore—or more likely never heard of—the breathtaking Selkirk and Purcell Ranges, the next ranges to the west. Backcountry population is small, trails are short, rough, steep, and few, and roads, with the one exception of Highway 1, which crosses the Selkirk Range at Rogers Pass in Glacier National Park (Canadian), are bumpy and dirty. Each of the four trails described in Hike 42 is great.

Pacific Rim National Park

Pacific Rim National Park

39 ▪ West Coast Trail

DAY HIKE OR BACKPACK	BACKPACK
Michigan Creek	**Bamfield–Port Renfrew**
Round trip • 24 km (15 miles)	One way • 75 km (47 miles)
Hiking time • 8 hours	Hiking time • 5–8 days
High point • 91 m (300 feet)	High point • 190 m (625 feet)
Elevation gain • 91 m (300 feet)	Elevation gain • 396 m (1300 feet)
Hikable • all year	Hikable • mid-May to October

RESOURCES

Management • Pacific Rim National Park

Map • West Coast Trail

Hiker map • Obtain the West Coast Trail map from the Province of British Columbia; Map Production, Surveys and Mapping Branch, Ministry of The Environment, 553 Superior Street, Parliament Buildings, Victoria, British Columbia V8V 1X4; the map is not for sale in Port Alberni or at the trailheads

Information • The Superintendent, Pacific Rim National Park, Box 280, Ucluelet, British Columbia V0R 3A0; phone (604) 728-3234 (mid-May to September 30)

Permits • Voluntary registration

Protection status • Pacific Rim National Park

Since 1854 at least sixty ships attempting to enter the Strait of Juan de Fuca have been driven by storms onto a stretch of Vancouver Island's west coast known as the Graveyard of the Pacific. After the wreck of the *S.S. Valencia* in 1906 in which 126 people perished, the government built a trail to permit mariners lucky enough to get ashore to escape the wilderness on foot. Though new rescue methods ultimately eliminated the need, recreational hikers discovered the attractions of this 75-km (47-mile) route, which partly follows the beach, partly beats through forest jungle.

In 1970 the Lifesaving Trail (or Shipwreck Trail), now called the West Coast Trail, together with a buffer strip of forest, was placed in Pacific Rim National Park, the first national park on Canada's west coast. Other units of the park are Long Beach, north of Ucluelet, providing a few short trails for the casual hiker, and the Broken Group Islands, a kayaker's paradise.

The original trail has been upgraded with boardwalks through swamps and bridges or cable cars over all but two of the major river crossings; at these, Nitinat Narrows and Gordon River, reliable ferry service is offered, for a fee, by local Indians from mid-May through September.

The trail has become exceedingly popular, drawing hikers from several continents. The coastal scenery is one attraction. The challenge is another. Campsites beside creeks are plentiful, and driftwood for fires is abundant. Wildlife is also plentiful; bear, raccoons, and mice are common enough to be considered pests. Bald eagles nest in trees along the shore and sightings are frequent.

The suggested day hike presents no extraordinary difficulties of trailhead access.

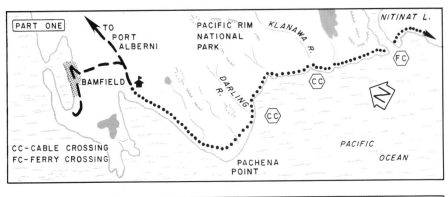

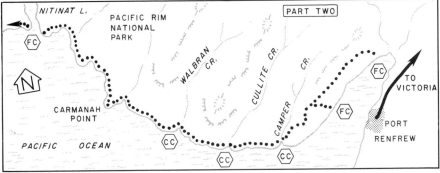

The backpack (the pounding surf and miles of forest give it its status as great) from Bamfield to Port Renfrew requires careful planning. A two-car swap may be arranged, with all the usual cumbersome complications. The alternative is (possibly) public transportation. The north end of the trail is at Pachena Bay (located 5 km [3 miles] from Bamfield), and reached by a 90-km (56-mile) dirt road from Port Alberni. (If driving, pick up a road guide at the Port Alberni tourist information center.) Public transportation can be used here; take the bus to Port Alberni, bus or boat to Bamfield, and walk the short distance to the trailhead. The south end is on the San Juan River near Port Renfrew, 106 km (66 miles) west of Victoria on paved Highway 14. This trailhead is on Indian reserve land and a fee is charged for parking. Port Renfrew has no public transportation, though in 1989 a private firm was attempting to run twice-daily limousine service from Victoria. Check with the park when you write for trail information.

Be well prepared for rain—the west coast of Vancouver Island receives 2692 mm (102 inches) a year. The terrain is so often unsmooth that sturdy leather hiking boots are recommended. Each party should carry a 15-m (45-foot) length of stout cord or rope for safeguarding crossings of surge channels in the surf and to expedite rescues when necessary. Be sure to carry a tide table and the West Coast Trail map, which gives exact information on shoreline routes and the tides at which beaches are passable.

The day hike samples only the first and easiest 12 km of the north end of the route. The opening 10 km from Pachena Bay Information Centre to Pachena Point Lighthouse (location also of a bed-and-breakfast) are on a wide trail. The next 2 km give a taste of what lies ahead. The trail narrows and descends a muddy hillside to Michigan Creek, a great base for beach exploration at low tide. Above high-tide level on both sides of the creek are excellent campsites; to get one arrive plenty early in the day.

South of Michigan Creek the going is slow on cobblestone beaches, equally slow on narrow, slippery trails, and slower yet on the steep ladders that climb headlands. The backpack is no trip for any but the physically sturdy and the wilderness-experienced. A weak or novice party is almost certain to get in trouble and when it does, help will be a long time coming.

But all is not agony and terror. Between traumas are joys the greater for the price paid. The ocean-side scenery is superb. Tide pools demand exploration. Bald eagles call for attention from their roosts high in wind-tortured trees at the water's edge. Grebes, cormorants, loons, great blue herons, and black oystercatchers keep the most casual birder fascinated.

Highlights of the first half of the hike include: the cable-car across the Darling River near 14 km, the Tsocowis Creek waterfall at 17 km, the cable-car crossing of Klanawa River at 23 km, Tsusiat Falls near 25 km, the beach walk from Tsusiat Falls to Tsuquadra Point, including a passage through a rock arch near 27 km, and the ferry across the Nitinat Narrows at 32.5 km. Hikers who do not wish to cope with the car-shuffle can turn around at the Narrows knowing they have sampled some of the best of the coast.

Highlights of the second half of the route include: returning to the beach at 36 km after being inland, the Carmanah Lighthouse at 44 km, the delightful cable-car ride over Carmanah Creek at 46 km, the beach walk from Carmanah Point to Vancouver Point at 51 km, the cable-car crossing of Walbran Creek at 53 km, the cable-car crossings of Cullite Creek at 58 km and Camper Creek at 62 km, and the beach hike around Owen Point to Thrasher Cove at 70 km. The final 5 km are on a hillside overlooking the Port San Juan channel, where the trail heads east to the Gordon River and the final ferry.

Tsusiat River ends in a waterfall on the ocean beach

40 ▪ Garibaldi Lake–Black Tusk Meadows

DAY HIKE

Garibaldi Lake

Round trip • 18 km (11 miles)
Hiking time • 10 hours
High point • 1470 m (4820 feet)
Elevation gain • 1060 m (3450 feet)

BACKPACK

Garibaldi Lake–Black Tusk Meadows

Round trip • 41 km (25 miles)
Hiking time • 2 days
High point • 2100 m (6880 feet)
Elevation gain • 1500 m (4940 feet)

RESOURCES

Hikable • July to mid-October
Management • Garibaldi Provincial Park
Topographical map • North Section Garibaldi Provincial Park
Hiker map • Free handout—topographical map best
Information • Ministry of Parks, Alice Lake Provincial Park, Box 220, Brackendale,
 British Columbia V0N 1H0; phone (604) 898-3678
Protection status • Garibaldi Provincial Park

Highlights of lake, meadows, and glaciers can be sampled in a single long day; doing every trail and exploring the kilometers of meadow take several days. Camping is luxurious. After hiking 10 km one is surprised to pay so high a camping fee, but then, one is surprised by the fancy kitchens, propane stoves, and leveled tentsites—all with a million-dollar view of Garibaldi Lake and glaciers.

Drive Highway 99 from North Vancouver around Howe Sound to the stoplight at Squamish. Continue on Highway 99 another 33 km (20 miles) and go right 2.4 km (1.5 miles) to the Garibaldi–Black Tusk parking lot, elevation 600 m (1950 feet).

The trail switchbacks up a superb ancient forest of firs and cedars, at 3.5 km entering Black Tusk Nature Conservancy/Garibaldi Provincial Park. Still in trees, at about 6 km the trail forks. For the closest camping, go left on a 1-km sidetrip to Taylor Creek Campground, 1500 m, 7.25 km from the road. The right fork passes a viewpoint of The Barrier cliffs and two small lakes. At 9 km from the road is awesome Garibaldi

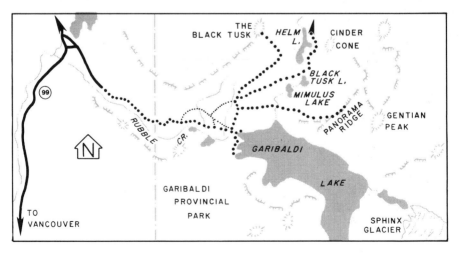

Garibaldi Lake and Mount Garibaldi

Lake, 1470 m. Follow the path to the right for picnic tables protected from the elements and lakeside campsites for the backpacker. This is an excellent base for a day or two of exploring.

Though the lake is the turnaround point for a day hike, if time permits a visit should be made to the flower gardens of Black Tusk Meadows, adding 3 km of distance and 200 m of elevation. Walk back to the lake outlet and go straight ahead, climbing to meadows below the pinnacle of well-named Black Tusk. In a long 2 km is a junction, 1650 m. Day-trippers go left down 2 km of meadow, past Taylor Creek Campground, and back to the parking lot at the road-end.

For those staying a day or two, from the junction in Black Tusk Meadows two trails set off uphill. The first climbs 3.25 km to the top of 2100-m Panorama Ridge and grand views of Garibaldi Lake, mountains, and enormous glaciers.

Here the visitor gazes not only far across the geographical present but far into the geological past. Many of the area's volcanoes were active during the height of the Ice Age, so that their flows of hot lava, instead of spreading out horizontally, were pressed against solid ice, resulting in almost vertical walls of basalt. The unusually steep walls of Mt. Garibaldi and the Black Tusk are examples, and at the head of the lake is a black cliff with a window like the eye of a needle. The Garibaldi Lake basin was scooped by Ice Age glaciers; successors still come almost to the shore. The Cinder Flats are the result of more recent eruptions, as are the flower fields richly nourished by fertile volcanic soils.

The second uphill trail splits, the left fork climbing steeply 3.25 km up the green side of the Black Tusk to an excellent viewpoint, the right fork traversing alongside the Helm Glacier past the Cinder Flats, Black Tusk Lake, and Mimulus Lake 3.5 km to Helm Lake, 1750 m. It continues 11 km to Cheakamus Lake, 914 m, only 3.25 km from the road-end near Whistler.

41 ▪ Cathedral Lakes

DAY HIKES
Six from Quiniscoe Lake basecamp

BACKPACK
Quiniscoe Lake as basecamp
Round trip • 16 km (10 miles)
Hiking time • 8 hours
High point • 2050 m (6700 feet)
Elevation gain • 1325 m (4318 feet) in,
175 m (575 feet) out

RESOURCES
Hikable • July to mid-October
Management • Cathedral Provincial Park
Map • NTS Ashnola River 92 H/1
Hiker maps • Outdoor Recreation Maps of British Columbia #8 (Princeton–Manning–Cathedral Region), B.C. Parks Cathedral Provincial Park Map
Information • Ministry of Parks, District Manager, Box 318, Summerland, British Columbia V0H 1Z0; phone (604) 494-0321
Protection status • Cathedral Lakes Provincial Park

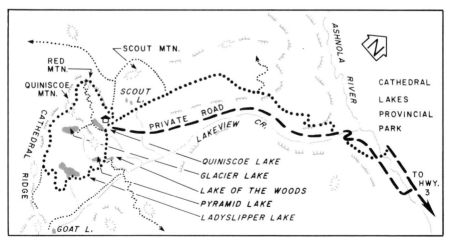

Jeep service by Cathedral Lakes Resort is responsible for the sweatfree access to a remote backcountry that would otherwise be true wilderness. Visitors stay either at the Quiniscoe Lake lodge or one of three nearby backcountry camp areas (nightly fee). The transportation is expensive and reservations must be made in advance. Write to Cathedral Lakes Resort Limited, RR1, Keremeos, British Columbia V0X 1N0, or telephone (604) 499-5848.

Thrifty folk who love a good hike or just dislike jeeps can walk into the Cathedral Lakes area via any of three excellent trails. The most-used is the 16-km (10-mile) High Trail, which gains 1325 m (4318 feet) from its start on the Ashnola River to its end at Quiniscoe Lake; an overnight camp at Lindsey Creek breaks that big chunk of elevation gain into two easy pieces. The Walls Creek access follows the Centennial Trail 20 km (12.5 miles), gaining 1200 m (3937 feet) to the lakes. The third access is the Ewart Creek trail, which follows the creek south to join the Centennial Trail before swinging west to cross high meadows to the lakes in 32 km (20 miles). Many hikers prefer to walk the jeep road, the shortest access of all. Park officials wish they wouldn't but don't insist.

Ladyslipper Lake and Cathedral Ridge

Quiniscoe Lake, Lakeview Mountain, and The Boxcar

Cathedral Provincial Park is reached by driving Highway 3 to Keremeos. If you have not already done so, pick up the provincial park brochure at the Tourist Information Centre. Head west, out of town, on Highway 3 for 3 km (2 miles) and turn south on the well-signed Ashnola River Road 22.7 km (14.2 miles) to the Base Camp, where the jeep road begins. If planning to walk the High Trail, continue 1.6 km (1 mile) to the Lakeview Creek Trailhead and Campground where a footbridge crosses the river, elevation 920 m (300 feet).

Whatever route is used, jeep or trail, the destination is Quiniscoe Lake, elevation 2050 m (6700 feet).

The center section of the park, encompassing the lakes and the high alpine area, is known as "the core." Due to heavy human impact, camping is restricted to three designated areas. Hiking, however, is unlimited on trails and well-marked routes. Inexperienced hikers should stick to the trails; the routes are often steep and rough, and require some navigation skills when the weather is poor. Favorite day hikes from Quiniscoe Lake follow.

Glacier Lake
Round trip • 3.2 km (2 miles)

From Quiniscoe Lake, walk through the camp area and go left over a low hill to the basin and subalpine lake.

Ladyslipper Lake
Round trip • 5 km (3.1 miles)

From Quiniscoe Lake, pass the forested Pyramid Lake and then head steeply up to high alpine meadows. Cross a low knoll and descend into a glacier-carved basin to delightful Ladyslipper Lake.

Goat Lakes
Round trip • 10 km (6.3 miles)

From Quiniscoe Lake, hike to Pyramid Lake and descend into the Lakeview Creek valley. The trail heads upvalley to the two subalpine lakes boxed in by towering walls of The Boxcar, Denture, and Cathedral Ridges.

Diamond Trail
Loop trip • 8 km (5 miles)

Beginning at Quiniscoe Lake, head north and traverse rich meadows while looping around Scout Mountain and the excellent views.

Stone City and the Rim Trail
Loop trip • 18 km (11.3 miles)

To get to this high alpine country, pass Glacier Lake, climb to the 2553-m (8376-foot) summit of Quiniscoe Mountain, and follow the Rim Trail to Stone City and big views. Descend past Ladyslipper and Pyramid Lakes to complete the loop.

Lakeview Mountain
Round trip • 14 km (8.7 miles)

Excellent views of the Cathedral Lakes and Haystack Mountain await at the 2628-m (8622-foot) summit of Lakeview Mountain.

Golden-mantled ground squirrel

42 ▪ Lake of the Hanging Glacier and Other Hikes

FOUR DAY HIKES

RESOURCES

Hikable • July to mid-October
Topographical maps • Listed in text
Hiker map • Free handout; topographical maps are best
Information • Ministry of Forest, Box 189, Invermere, British Columbia V0A 1K0;
    phone (604) 342-4200; for Glacier National Park trails, P.O. Box 350,
    Revelstoke, British Columbia V0E 2S0; phone (604) 837-5155
Protection status • Unprotected
Note: Local maps and information are given in a mixture of *feet* and *meters*

Mountain climbers long have known the massive icefields, vigorous glaciers, and rugged peaks. It was to serve them that Glacier House was built near Rogers Pass in 1880 by the Canadian Pacific Railroad and the first alpine guide service in the New World established. The operation was abandoned 40 years later in favor of developments at Banff and Lake Louise, and since then all but several areas of the Selkirks have been virtually left alone by man. Except at one or two spots, the adjoining Purcells (considered by some geographers to be a subrange of the Selkirks) never did receive more than cursory attention. Until, that is, the arrival of the helicopter.

If a single hike is to be made, it should be, must be, to the Lake of the Hanging Glacier described below. To experience all the range has to offer would take weeks, with a variety of forest, lakes, meadows, and maybe solitude, exploring all the short trails

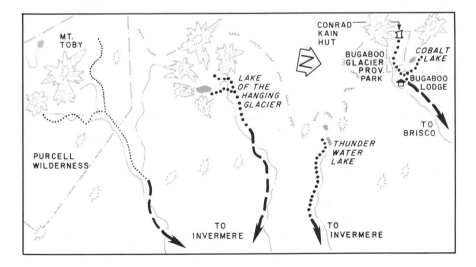

Lake of the Hanging Glacier

on day hikes or backpacks, including the 20-km Toby Glacier Trail recommended by a B.C. forester, but not hiked by the authors.

Peaks in the Sir Donald group of the Selkirks, in Glacier National Park, are spectacular, but though the trails have the advantage (unusual for the region) of beginning from paved roads, they are short and steep, deadending at glaciers or rock walls, very discouraging to backpackers. Should a party of hikers nevertheless decide on a ridge-top sunrise, a backcountry permit is required, obtainable from the warden's office directly across the highway from the Glacier National Park Information Centre. The following hikes are described north to south.

Abbott Ridge
Round trip • 13 km (7¹/₂ miles)   Elevation gain • 1040 m (3380 feet)
High point • 2454 m (8050 feet)   Maps • Mount Revelstoke, Glacier
                                                    National Park

A steady ascent, steep much of the way, to a 360-degree view of glaciers and mountains, forest and flowers.

From Rogers Pass Information Centre drive west 4 km (2.4 miles) and turn left on the Illecillewaet Campground road. Drive 1.6 km (1 mile) past the campground and the first trailhead to the road-end at the Glacier House Memorial, elevation 1250 m.

The trail starts flat. In 100 m go right and turn steeply upward through a coastal-type forest that yields to subalpine, which in turn yields at 3 km to alpine flowers and mosses. The views expand. At 2.2 km is Marion Lake in a basin excavated by ancient glaciers. Continue up to avoid a steep snowfield that lasts through most of the summer. At the first junction, keep right, ever upward, to the 2454-m crest of Abbott Ridge and the famous view of Mt. Sir Donald, the Illecillewaet Neve, and, below, laid out like a map, Rogers Pass, Highway 1, and the west portals of the two Canadian Pacific tunnels.

Conrad Kain Hut
Round trip • 10 km (6 miles)   Elevation gain • 700 m (2275 feet)
High point • 2238 m (8100 feet)   Maps • 82 K/10, 82 K/15

The Conrad Kain Hut is located at the 2238-m (8100-foot) level below Bugaboo Spire in the Purcells. The hovel has room for 50 humans who pay an overnight fee for the pleasure of being packed like sardines. Better to carry a tent or day-hike.

Drive Highway 95 north of Radium to Brisco and turn west 48 km (29 miles) on a dusty, rough road to a junction. The left fork leads to the Canadian Mountain Holidays Bugaboo Lodge and public campground. Take the right fork 4 km (2.4 miles) to the Bugaboo Glacier trailhead, elevation 1538 m (5000 feet).

The first 1.5 km is a fairly level forest walk. The trail then tilts skyward, gaining 700 m in the next 4 km to the views.

Cobalt (Blue) Lake Trail
Round trip • 3 km (1³/₄ mile)   Elevation gain • 884 m (2870 feet)
High point • 2422 m (7900 feet)   Maps • 82 K/10, 82 K/15

The trail starts at Bugaboo Lodge, crosses the Bugaboo Glacier road (no place to park here), and climbs steeply to larch-scattered alpine meadows with views of the Bugaboo

Mount Sir Donald from Abbott Ridge trail

Glacier and the ice-clad Quintel Peaks. The trail ends on a ridge top: From there a hiker must find his own way to Cobalt Lake.

Lake of the Hanging Glacier

Round trip • 14 km (9 miles)   Elevation gain • 675 m (2200 feet)
High point • 2154 m (7000 feet)   Maps • 82 K/7, 82 K/10

The most exciting trail in the Purcells leads to a 2.5-km-long (1½-mile-long) lake beneath glacier-carved walls of the Commander Mountains, whose glaciers flow into the lake, littering the milky ice water with icebergs.

South of Radium 16 km (10 miles) on Highway 93/95, turn west 3 km (1.8 miles) toward Invermere. Cross the Columbia River and just beyond the railroad tracks go north on a road signed "Wilmer" and "Panorama." In 1.7 km (1.1 miles) from that junction cross Toby Creek. At 4 km (2.5 miles) drive through Wilmer on Main Street, which becomes the West Side Road. At 14 km (8.4 miles) from Invermere go left on the Horsethief Creek road (unsigned) some 40 km (27 miles) to the road-end, elevation 1477 m (4800 feet).

The abandoned road has been converted into excellent trail 3 km to a bridge over Horsethief Creek at 1650 m. Switchbacks then climb to campsites near the shore of the lake, 2154 m. Steep cliffs put further exploration in the realm of mountain climbers.

Thunderwater Lake

Round trip • 12 km (7 miles)   Elevation gain • 370 m (1200 feet)
High point • 2150 m (7000 feet)   Map • 82 K/10

If time permits, Thunderwater Lake also is worth the hike. Drive Horsethief Creek road 5.8 km (3.5 miles) and go right 26.5 km (17.5 miles) on Forester Creek road. (The last 0.8 km [0.4 mile] can only be managed by a high-clearance vehicle.) The road ends at a washed-out bridge.

Cross the creek and go upstream on an abandoned brush-covered road about 2 km to a second stream, ford it, and hike 100 m in forest to a cabin near the edge of meadowland. From here the trail is lost and one must follow the stream to the lake.

Clark's nutcracker

CANADIAN ROCKIES

Not to belittle the south-of-the-border prelude, in Canada the Rocky Mountains achieve their climax. So enormous is the staggering quantity of scenic wealth that most of the range has been blithely delivered to loggers and stripminers and dammers. Luckily, though, decades before exploiters arrived in force one of North America's grandest systems of parks already had been dedicated. Conservationists working to achieve proper protection for the rest of the Canadian Rockies are consoled and inspired by the continuous parkland 250 miles long and 20–60 miles wide.

The beauties are easily seen. The Banff–Jasper Highway is one breathtaking experience after another and tourists not totally jaded by roadside views can ride snowmobiles up the Columbia Icefield, gondolas to fabulous panoramas; helicopters, more's the shame, clatter the skies everywhere.

Why bother to hike, then? Because from a machine one may *see* but never deeply *feel*. Despite roads, despite fame, the Canadian Rockies are so vast the walker can find whatever degree of private quiet he seeks. For those who want a little, plus comforts unusual for wildland pedestrians in the Western Hemisphere, there are backcountry lodges patterned after the Swiss Alps. For those who want as much as they can get, there are long trails into wilderness defended against casual entry by wide and violent and unbridged rivers.

The climbers who flock by the thousands from around the world crowd only a few mountains, leaving hundreds of others alone. Most of the great routes are mainly or entirely on ice, some very steep; the sedimentary structures by and large are too loose to satisfy refined tastes.

Hiking ordinarily gets underway in the second half of June and continues through October. June is often cold and clear but can be steadily miserable. July and August are generally fair and hot with frequent afternoon thunderstorms; an occasional summer is rainy from start to end. Some Augusts the sky is obscured by smoke and about one year in three all trails are closed by fire danger; other times travel is permitted but campfires banned. September and early October frequently offer the best hiking, the days bright and the nights freezing.

As seen from Magog Lake, Mt. Assiniboine, the centerpiece of Mount Assiniboine Provincial Park, is almost an identical twin to Europe's Matterhorn. In addition, the view from Magog Lake (Hike 43) offers alpine lakes, glaciers, and much more.

Icebergs drift on Floe Lake, surrounded by cliffs and glaciers. Four major passes and gorgeous meadows make Hike 44, the Rockwall Pass loop in Kootenay National Park, the greatest in the Vermilion Range.

Banff National Park is the most famous and most popular national park in Canada. Fortunately, most tourists spend their time shopping for gewgaws and sipping tea, so most trails are no more crowded, even less so, than most wilderness areas in the states. The Lake Minnewanka trail (Hike 45) has broad meadows and three lakes to traverse.

Healy Pass (Hike 46) and the Skoki Trail (Hike 48) are noted for wildflowers and views of glacier-covered peaks. Only the Plain-of-the-Six-Glaciers (Hike 47) is truly mobbed, but the scenery is so spectacular it is worth putting up with a crowd for a day.

Thundering waterfalls, wispy waterfalls, and just ordinary waterfalls are the leading attraction of Little Yoho Valley (Hike 49) of Yoho National Park, but there is much more—forest, icefields, glaciers, and mountains. Lake O'Hara (Hike 50) offers alpine lakes, meadows, and spectacular peaks.

In Jasper National Park, hundreds of miles of trails lead to forested valleys, vast flower fields, mountain lakes, glacier-clad mountains, and views of the Columbia Icefield, largest in the Canadian Rockies.

Nigel Pass (Hike 51) starts in Banff National Park and climbs to views of the

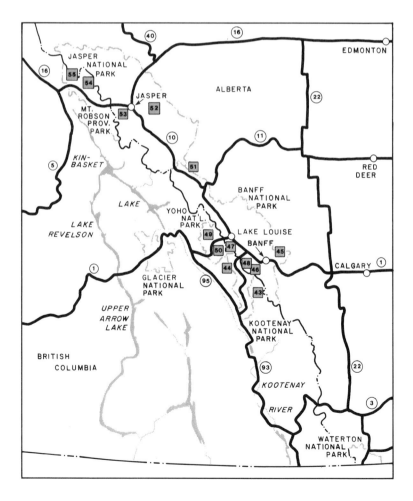

Twin Falls

Columbia Icefield, alpine meadows, and a mountain lake. Skyline Trail (Hike 52) is, as the name suggests, a sky-high ridge walk through flower fields and tundra-type vegetation, while the Tonquin Valley (Hike 53) has been proclaimed a miniature Shangri-La with spectacular lakes, spectacular mountains, and miles of spectacular meadows. The North Boundary Trail (Hike 54) is a hundred-mile-long wilderness trail for those who want to be alone. It goes deep into the northern Rockies, first in forest, then climbing to meadowland, and finally reaching a climax at Robson Pass and the glaciers of Mt. Robson.

In Mount Robson Provincial Park, blocks of ice tumbling from the Tumbling Glacier give Berg Lake its name. Hike 55 winds through forest, past numerous waterfalls, to the lake below Mt. Robson, highest in the Canadian Rockies.

43 ▪ Magog Lake

DAY HIKE	BACKPACK
None	**Magog Lake**

Round trip • 54 km (34 miles)
Hiking time • 5 days
High point • 2423 m (7950 feet)
Elevation gain • 723 m (2350 feet)

RESOURCES

Hikable • late June through September
Management • Mount Assiniboine Provincial Park
Topographical maps • Mt. Assiniboine 82 J/13, Spray Lakes Reservoir 82 J/14
Hiker maps • Use the topographical maps
Information • Banff National Park, Box 900, Banff, Alberta T0L 0C0; phone (403)
    762-4256
Protection status • Mount Assiniboine Provincial Park

The similarity of Mt. Assiniboine as viewed from Magog Lake to Switzerland's
Matterhorn is striking. All that's missing is the little red train carrying tourists up to
the Gonergrat. There are no tourist hordes here, but the views and wildflowers assure
that a hiker will always have company. The peaks, the lakes, the forests, and the rolling
meadows add up to four of the six requirements for greatness, enough to compensate
for the impossibility of solitude and the improbability of animals. Three trails, none
easy, lead to Magog Lake. The one described here is the most scenic.

Drive Highway 1 to the most northerly Canmore exit and follow 2nd Avenue 1.9
km (1.2 miles). Turn right on 17th Street 0.6 km (0.4 mile), then left on Fairholm
(which turns into 8th Avenue) 1 km (0.6 mile) to Rundle Avenue. Proceed on Rundle
until it becomes Bridge Avenue, cross the Bow River, and follow signs to Spray Lakes
Reservoir, the road soon deteriorating to rough gravel. At 12.3 km (7.6 miles) cross
the dam and continue around the lakes, the road more difficult with each kilometer.
At 16 km (9.9 miles) from the dam is a parking area at the lakes' overflow, usually dry;

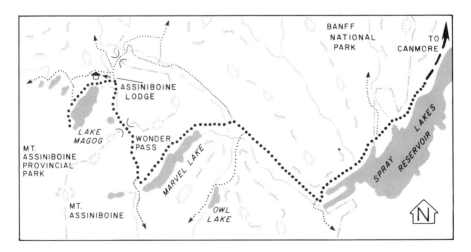

elevation 1700 m (5600 feet). The road continues 6.4 km (4 miles) but unless the vehicle is four-wheel drive it is better to walk.

Walk across the spillway and follow the jeep track past a gated service road from Banff. At 6.4 km is a horse ranch and the start of true trail at the entry to Banff National Park. Keep right at the first junction, following Bryant Creek upstream on a gentle rise. At 11 km from the spillway pass the Owl Lake trail. Several campsites are at 13.5 km. Bryant Creek Warden Station is situated by a split in the trail. The right fork over Assiniboine Pass is shorter but the views are more spectacular over Wonder Pass, so grumble about crazy guidebook authors and go left, climbing above the blue-green water of Marvel Lake to vistas of the icefield below Aye Mountain. Long switchbacks in flower-covered meadows cross 2423-m Wonder Pass at 22.5 km from Spray Lakes Spillway. An easy descent past the Naiset Cabins, warden's cabin, and Assiniboine Lodge leads to Magog Lake campsites, 3240 m, 27 km from the overflow.

Most hikers will take a day simply to gape at the view from camp before setting out for a day or two wandering nearby trails. For variety, the return trip can be made over 2177-m Assiniboine Pass and down the forested valley of Bryant Creek to Spray Lakes.

Assiniboine Lodge, Lake Magog, and Mount Assiniboine

44 • Vermilion Range—Floe Lake–Rockwall Pass Loop

DAY HIKE	BACKPACK
Floe Lake	**Rockwall Pass Loop**
Round trip • 19.2 km (12 miles)	One way • 46.7 km (29½ miles)
Hiking time • 7 hours	Hiking time • 4–5 days
High point • 2055 m (6700 feet)	High point • 2392 m (7800 feet)
Elevation gain • 705 m (2300 feet)	Elevation gain • 2990 m (9844 feet)

RESOURCES

Hikable • July through September
Management • Kootenay National Park
Map • NTS Mt. Goodsir 82 N/1
Hiker map • Banff, Kootenay and Yoho National Parks topo
Information • Superintendent, Kootenay National Park, Box 220, Radium Hot
    Springs, British Columbia V0A 1M0; phone (604) 347-9551
Permits • Required for overnight hikes
Protection status • Kootenay National Park

The day hike to Floe Lake, a flotilla of icebergs drifting its surface and cliffs leaping above to snowy-icy peaks, is so popular that a reservation must be made early to spend a night at the lake. The lake is the first stage of the backpack (satisfying three of the six criteria for greatness—scenery, creeks and a lake, and flowers). Rockwall Pass loop along the east slopes of the Vermilion Range is not only the best hike in Kootenay National Park but one of the finest in the Canadian Rockies, a traverse of four major passes, beside glaciers, across jumbled moraines, and through gorgeous meadows. The route starts by climbing to Floe Lake, then heads northwest over Numa Pass, Tumbling Pass, Rockwall Pass, and Limestone Pass before descending Helmet and Ochre Creeks to the end on Highway 93, 14.4 km (9 miles) by road from the start. Be prepared for a knee-wet creek crossing.

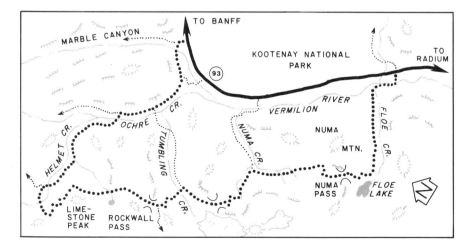

Floe Lake

Drive Highway 93 south from the Banff–Kootenay Parks boundary 21.6 km (13.4 miles) or north 8.2 km (5.1 miles) from Vermilion Crossing. Park in the gravel lot on the west side of the highway, elevation 1335 m (4380 feet).

The journey begins with an 0.8-km stroll along the Vermilion River valley, crossing the river and Floe Creek on sturdy footbridges. The trail then gets down to serious business, steeply switchbacking up the forested flank of Numa Mountain to a leveling-off in Floe Creek Valley. At 7.2 km, still in the valley, is the first campsite, just before the start of a second series of steep switchbacks. At 9.6 km are a small meadow above Floe Lake and the first official lake campsites. Several others are near the warden's cabin. The sampler hike turns around here.

Tumbling Glacier

The traverse climbs from the lake a scant 2 km in larch forest to meadows and Numa Pass, 2392 m, and views of Foster Peak, Numa Mountain, and a host of nameless peaks and icefields.

The trail is faint at the pass but soon becomes distinct on the steep descent of the north side through meadows, over moraines, into forest. At 8.8 km from Floe Lake is Numa Creek backcountry campsite, 1534 m, and a junction. Stay left and begin the steep ascent 4.8-km to Tumbling Pass, 2269 m.

The trail drops 2.8 km from the pass to Tumbling Creek trail junction, 1901 m. Continue straight on the Rockwall Pass trail a scant 0.4 km beyond the junction to a backcountry campsite. The trail steepens, switchbacking to high meadows at 1.6 km from Tumbling Creek. To the right is Wolverine Pass and a warden's cabin. Continue straight ahead, ascending gradually to the summit of Rockwall Pass, 2269 m, 4 km from Tumbling Creek junction. The trail disappears occasionally but the route is well marked by cairns and poles.

The 1.6-km descent from the pass ends at a swiftly flowing, glacier-fed creek, 1963 m. This water is very cold and there is no bridge. Your feet probably are going to get wet and blue. The crossing is a little easier upstream where the creek is not so deep. Shortly beyond is a backcountry camp on a knoll overlooking the creek.

The trail climbs open meadow to the pass, 2173 m, on a shoulder of Limestone Peak, 7.2 km from Tumbling Creek junction. The trail then descends Helmet Creek 4 km, passing a warden's cabin, backcountry camp, and views of Helmet Falls. The camp is an excellent staging ground for a 3.2-km sidetrip to Goodsir Pass and big views of glaciers and rock spires.

At 11.8 km from Tumbling Creek the Rockwall Pass trail ends. Straight ahead is the trail to Goodsir Pass. Go right, down Helmet Creek trail. At 7.6 km from the Rockwall Pass trail, pass a forested backcountry campsite and cross Ochre Creek. The Helmet Creek trail officially ends at a junction. To the left is the poorly maintained Ottertail Pass trail. Go right on the Ochre Creek trail the final, nearly level 6.4 km to the Marble Canyon parking area and the offical end of the trail. The trail may be left 1.6 km earlier at the Paint Pots area, putting you only 12.8 km by road from the start.

Warden's cabin at Floe Lake

45 ▪ Lake Minnewanka—Aylmer Lookout– Devils Gap

DAY HIKE
Aylmer Lookout
Round trip • 26.4 km (16¹/₂ miles)
Hiking time • 8 hours
High point • 2252 m (7400 feet)
Elevation gain • 791 m (2600 feet)
Hikable • July to mid-October
Map • NTS Lake Minnewanka 82 O/6 W

BACKPACK
Devils Gap
Round trip • 56.8 km (34 miles)
Hiking time • 3 days
High point • 1461 m (4800 feet)
Elevation gain • none
Hikable • mid-July to September
Maps • NTS Lake Minnewanka 82 O/6 E and W, Canmore 82 O/3

RESOURCES
Management • Banff National Park
Hiker map • Banff, Kootenay, and Yoho National Parks topo
Information • Superintendent, Banff National Park, Box 900 Banff, Alberta T0L 0C0; phone (403) 762-4256
Permits • Required for overnight hikes
Protection status • Banff National Park

Among the most idyllic hikes in Banff National Park is the Lake Minnewanka trail along the north shore to vistas of the fiordlike lake and the Palliser Range towering above. Virgin forests, the lake, the spectacular views, and some flower meadows add up to four "great" characteristics; there's a chance of a fifth—mountain sheep. Six grassy campsites on the lakeshore are bathed by cooling breezes that keep temperatures comfortable and mosquitoes at bay. Day hikes along the shore are excellent samplers in themselves; the more strenuous climb to Aylmer Lookout is unsurpassed for vistas of lake and peaks. A saltlick maintained in the lookout area by wardens frequently treats hikers to close looks at bighorn sheep. The longer trip to Devils Gap is highly recommended as a backpack fit for novice and experienced hikers alike.

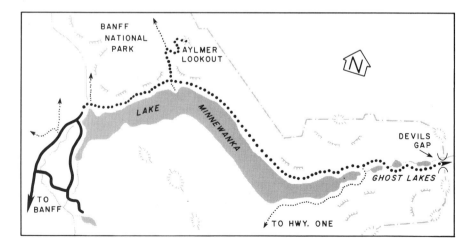

Lake Minnewanka from Aylmer Lookout trail

From the Banff Information Centre near the corner of Wolf and Banff Streets drive east on Banff Street, under Highway 1, and 10.4 km (6.5 miles) to the Lake Minnewanka parking area, elevation 1461 m (4800 feet).

Both the day hike and backpack begin on the Lake Minnewanka trail. From the parking lot walk past the boat dock and through the picnic area. When the road splits, stay left. The road soon yields to wide, gravel trail along the shore, diverging occasionally to skirt deep canyons that slice the hillside.

At 7.6 km the trail divides, giving a choice for the day hike. The left fork climbs to Aylmer Lookout, the middle trail continues up to the lake, and the right fork drops to the Aylmer Campsite on the shore. Be sure your water bottles are full before starting up the steep forests of Aylmer Lookout trail. At 3.6 km from the lake a spur branches left and down to a waterhole. Shortly beyond this spur the trail divides again. Stay right;

the left fork heads to Aylmer Pass, then out of the park. At 5.2 km from the lake enter open meadows and switchback to the lookout, 2252 m.

If aiming for Devils Gap, from the lookout trail junction at 7.6 km continue straight ahead on the shore. Campsites are at 8.8, 9.6, 13.6, 17.6, and 18.4 km from the parking area. The path rounds the upper end of Lake Minnewanka and proceeds upvalley to Ghost Lakes. Between the first and second lakes the trail crosses a wide, shallow river channel to a campsite on the gravel bar. Beyond the second and third lakes is broad, open Devils Gap, 28.3 km. Here is the park boundary; the trail that continues is unmaintained and used mainly by horsepackers.

46 ▪ Healy Pass–Whistling Pass Loop

DAY HIKE	BACKPACK
Healy Pass	**Whistling Pass Loop**
Round trip • 17.6 km (11 miles)	Round trip • 51 km (32 miles)
Hiking time • 6 hours	Hiking time • 3–5 days
High point • 2313 m (7600 feet)	High point • 2313 m (7600 feet)
Elevation gain • 384 m (1260 feet)	Elevation gain • 1439 m (4720 feet)
Hikable • late June to September	Hikable • mid-July to September

RESOURCES

Management • Banff National Park
Map • NTS Banff 82 O/4 West
Hiker map • Banff, Kootenay, and Yoho National Parks topo
Information • Superintendent, Banff National Park, Box 900, Banff, Alberta T0L 0C0; phone (403) 762-4256
Permits • Required for overnight hikes
Protection status • Banff National Park

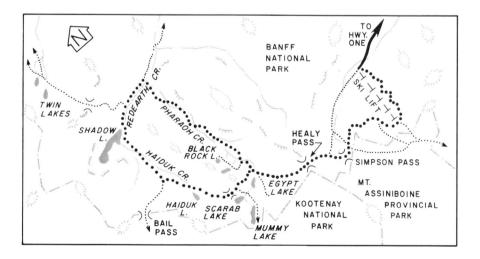

Scarab Lake and Egypt Lake (below) from Healy Pass

Alpine tarns, wildflowers, meadows, valley forests, and exceptional views combine to make Healy Pass an unforgettable great hike. No tour of the Canadian Rockies should be considered complete without a hike here.

Both the day hike and backpack begin with a gondola ride to the Sunshine Village Ski Area, then head across high meadows to Healy Pass. Because the trail offers no campsites, most hikers do the trip in a single (long) day. A loop trip, with camping options, can be made by returning on the less scenic Healy Creek trail. (*Note:* In 1989 some sections of the Healy Pass trail were closed temporarily for environmental reasons. Check beforehand with the Banff Information Centre.)

The backpack is an outstanding loop from Healy Pass around the rugged Pharaoh Peaks, wandering through one alpine meadow after another, passing one alpine lake after another. Numerous sidetrails lead to more lakes, enticing reasons to add extra exploring days to the trip.

Drive Highway 1 north from Banff townsite 8 km (5 miles) to the Sunshine Village Ski Area turnoff. Go west 11.2 km (7 miles) to the gondola parking lot, 1704 m (5591 feet). The final 5.6 km (3.5 miles) of road to the ski area are closed to public wheels. During the summer the gondola carries hikers there. Check at the Banff Information Centre for up-to-date schedules and fees. If on a tight budget you may prefer to walk the road.

The trail to Healy Pass begins at the northwest corner of the resort complex, 2191 m (7188 feet), and climbs the ski runs to a vast meadow. Cross a low saddle at

Haiduk Lake and Mount Ball

2.4 km and descend gradually to forested Simpson Pass, 2100 m. The trail then rolls along the sidehill 0.8 km before settling into a steady climb through broad meadow-lands. At 7.2 km is an intersection with the Healy Creek trail. Stay left and continue to climb lush alpine meadows to 2313-m Healy Pass at 8.8 km. Spend some time here filling your eyes. Egypt, Scarab, and Pharaoh Lakes nestle below the Pharaoh Peaks. On a clear day Mt. Assiniboine may be spotted to the southeast.

If you wish to make the Healy Pass sampler hike a loop, retrace steps from the pass 1.6 km and follow the Healy Creek trail down the valley to the gondola parking lot. The camp area, complete with picnic tables at each site and a backcountry toilet, is located 2.2 km down the Healy Creek trail.

For the longer loop descend from Healy Pass toward Egypt Lake, reaching the Whistling Pass Loop trail at 12 km from Sunshine Village Ski Area. The hikers' shelter and Egypt Lake backcountry campsite are a short distance to the left.

To save the best for last, do the loop counterclockwise. Head down Pharaoh Creek valley on a trail that swings back and forth across the creek eight times, on the way passing a rarely used campsite. At 9.5 km from the Healy Pass trail cross Redearth Creek to intersect the Redearth Creek trail and go left up Redearth Creek 2.8 km to Shadow Lake meadows, site of a camp area and the old Brewster Cabin. The Gibbon Pass trail taking off from Brewster Cabin is a highly recommended all-day sidetrip to Twins Lakes.

Beyond the camp area the route splits several times. Go straight across the meadow, following the most-used trail 1.2 km to the lower end of Shadow Lake, 1841 m. Beyond the lake the trail skirts a large, muddy meadow to a camp area at the Ball Pass trail junction, 16.7 km from the Healy Pass trail. Stay left over a forested knoll to Haiduk Lake. The trail ascends high alpine meadows, attaining the loop's high point, 2283 m at Whistling Pass, 22.5 km from the Healy Pass trail.

A kilometer beyond Whistling Pass a trail branches off on the right to Scarab Lake and beautiful Mummy Lake (both lakes are visible from the loop trail). Stay left for a short uphill stretch, then descend steeply to close the loop below Egypt Lake at 27 km. Several sidetrips start hereabouts; better plan to camp at least two nights. At 0.4 km below the camp area the trail to Pharaoh, Black Rock, and Sphinx Lakes takes off on the right for a scenic 8-km round trip. Natalko Lake is another sidetrip option; the trail is poorly maintained so be sure to carry a map for this 8.8-km excursion.

Mountain goat

47 ▪ Lake Louise

DAY HIKE

Lake Louise and Plain-of-the-Six-Glaciers
Round trip • 14.4 km (9 miles)
Hiking time • 5 hours
High point • 2187 m (7000 feet)
Elevation gain • 406 m (1300 feet)

BACKPACK

None

RESOURCES

Hikable • July to September
Management • Banff National Park
Map • NTS Lake Louise 82 N/8 West
Hiker map • Banff, Kootenay, and Yoho National Parks topo
Information • Superintendent, Banff National Park, Box 900, Banff, Alberta T0L 0C0; phone (403) 762-4256
Protection status • Banff National Park

Don't come to the most famous spot in the Canadian Rockies in search of solitude. The view from the parking lot and nearby Lake Louise draws pilgrims from all over North America and several other continents and has been doing so for a hundred years. Though most folks stay beside the lake, enough saddle up shanks' mare to make Plain-of-the-Six-Glaciers trail the most popular in the Canadian Rockies. The hike begins near the regal Chateau Lake Louise (referred to by sniffy climbers as "The Penitentiary"), follows the lakeshore with the super-famous views to Mt. Victoria, and ascends to a teahouse and viewpoint overlooking the six glaciers. Who can resist? Although the distance is skimpy, the trail is long on scenery and flowers, and has the promise of yellow-bellied marmots, if not moose or elk.

Drive west from Highway 1 for 6 km (3.7 miles) toward Lake Louise and leave your car in the enormous parking lot, elevation 1716 m (5630 feet).

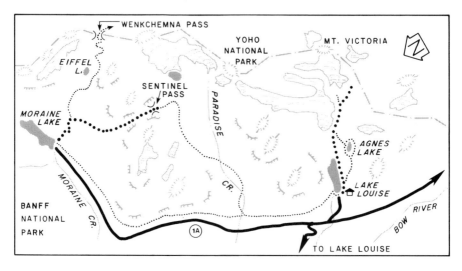

Teahouse and Lake Agnes

Walk the paved path between the chateau and the shore to a split at pavement's end. Proceed straight ahead around the north side of the lake; the right fork leads to Lake Agnes. At the lakehead the climb begins, ascending a little valley in forest of spruce and fir, then an ancient lateral moraine. At 4 km pass an unmarked trail to Lake Agnes.

At 4.8 km the Highline Trail branches off right, heading back toward Lake Agnes and the Beehives. Continue straight, switchbacking up open slopes below Mt. Whyte with excellent views of Mt. Victoria and the glaciers. The Plain-of-the-Six-Glaciers Teahouse, perched on a moraine bench, its backdoor up against a cliff, is reached at 5.5 km, 2088 m. Beverages and hot food are available. Beyond the teahouse the trail splits. The lesser-used path branches off right, climbing 305 m in 1.6 km to a breathtaking view of Mt. Victoria and the six glaciers. The main trail continues upvalley 0.4 km to the edge of the Victoria Glacier. The Highline Trail is an alternate, longer return to Chateau Lake Louise, touring the conical-shaped Beehives, Lake Agnes, and Mirror Lake.

For more hiking in the vicinity, try Moraine Lake. Drive from the town of Lake Louise 2 km (1.2 miles) and turn left 12.2 km (7.6 miles) to the road-end at another huge parking lot. Start in front of the lodge and walk southwest around Moraine Lake to a split in the trail. Stay right; the left fork parallels the lakeshore a short distance and ends. Climb steadily through open forest 3.2 km to an unmarked junction at 2270 m. The left fork goes to Eiffel Lake (an excellent destination) and the right climbs a small rise to Larch Valley.

Larch Valley offers superb roaming. Map in hand, wander through larch groves and open meadow to find two off-trail lakes. The wide valley climbs gently to the northwest, views improving with elevation. The most spectacular panorama is from 2600-m Sentinel Pass. The final climb to the pass is steep and exposed; don't try it if the trail is snowy.

48 ▪ The Skoki Trail— Ptarmigan Lake and the Fossil Mountain Loop

DAY HIKE
Ptarmigan Lake
Round trip • 16 km (10 miles)
Hiking time • 5 hours
High point • 2375 m (7600 feet)
Elevation gain • 325 m (1040 feet)
Hikable • mid-July to mid-October
Map • NTS Lake Louise 82 N/8

BACKPACK
Fossil Mountain Loop
Loop trip • 35 km (21³/₄ miles)
Hiking time • 3 days
High point • 2531 m (8100 feet)
Elevation gain • 728 m (2390 feet)
Hikable • mid-July to October
Maps • NTS Lake Louise 82 N/8,
   Hector Lake 82 N/9 East

RESOURCES
Management • Banff National Park
Hiker map • Banff, Kootenay, and Yoho National Parks topo
Information • Superintendent, Banff National Park, Box 900, Banff, Alberta T0L 0C0;
   phone (403) 762-4256
Permits • Required for overnight hikes
Protection status • Banff National Park

The arctic-alpine meadows, large tarns, and varied scenery of the Skoki area meet three of the six requirements for a great hike. There's a chance for a fourth—solitude—as the open country invites off-trail explorations of one day to many, tempting hikers to linger until the food runs out.

The day hike goes from the Lake Louise Ski Area over Boulder Pass to Ptarmigan Lake. Several nearby backcountry campsites permit easy extension to an overnighter. The Fossil Mountain Loop continues into the Slate Mountain Range, passing Skoki Lodge, Red Deer Lakes, and Baker Lake before returning to Ptarmigan Lake. Sidetrip possibilities are endless.

Drive Highway 1 to the southern Lake Louise townsite exit and turn east at the sign for "Gondola." Pass a road to the left, pass the Bow Valley Parkway to the right, and proceed uphill 1.8 km (1.2 miles). Turn right on a gravel road 1.1 km (0.7 miles) to the Fish Creek trailhead and park, elevation 1737 m (6000 feet). (Neither a Fish Creek nor a Fish Creek trail exist but the name is there just the same.)

Red Deer Lake and Oyster Peak

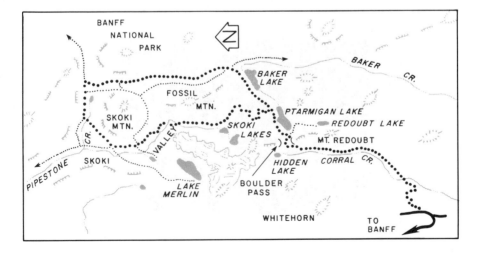

The hike begins on an uninspiring ski area road (open to area employees only), climbing steeply. In a fork at 0.8 km stay right. At 3.2 km, near the ski lodge, is a second split; take the upper road a short distance to its end and the start of actual trail, 2062 m.

After an abrupt straight-uphill start, the path climbs gradually from forest to lush alpine meadows. At 6.4 km is the Ptarmigan Hut (also called Halfway Ski Hut). Just beyond is an intersection with the Hidden Lake trail, leading northward to the lake in 1.2 km. From the junction the main trail climbs steadily to Boulder Pass, 2375 m. On a clear day the views are awesome, Mt. Temple and Mt. Victoria to the west and the Skoki area and Slate Mountains north, east, and south.

Ptarmigan Lake lies just over Boulder Pass at 8 km. Hikers who plan to spend the night must camp back down the trail near Ptarmigan Hut or continue to campsites at Redoubt Lake or Baker Lake.

The loop portion of the Fossil Mountain Loop begins when the trail splits at the northeast end of Ptarmigan Lake. Take the Skoki Trail on the left and climb arctic landscape to Deception Pass, 2531 m, 9.6 km from the ski area, and drop to the treeline and Skoki Valley. At 12.8 km the trail splits. Take the left, passing the Skoki Lodge at 14 km to the Skoki backcountry camp area at 14.5 km. Before continuing, take time for a 6.4-km sidetrip to Lake Merlin.

From the Skoki backcountry campsite descend the valley, skirting the base of Skoki Mountain. At 0.8 km the trail divides. Stay right 1.6 km to Little Pipestone Creek, 2093 m. Jump, wade, or search for a log to the north bank of the creek. At the edge of the forest find the Little Pipestone Creek trail. Head east (right) up a nearly flat valley to a warden's cabin and Red Deer River trail junction, 4 km from the Skoki backcountry campsite. The Red Deer River trail heads south. Just to the right is a path to the Red Deer Lakes backcountry campsite and the horsepackers' route to Skoki Lodge.

To complete the loop around Fossil Mountain, go south on the Red Deer River trail 5.6 km to the Baker Lake trail, which leads to Baker Lake and backcountry campsite. Nearby, Little Baker, Tilted, and Brachiopod Lakes offer excellent excuses to linger in the Baker Lake area. The loop portion of the hike is closed at Ptarmigan Lake, 2 km beyond the Baker Lake backcountry campsite. Go over the pass on the Skoki Trail and down through the ski area.

A friendly visitor

49 ▪ Little Yoho River Valley

DAY HIKE	BACKPACK
Twin Falls	**Little Yoho Loop**
Round trip • 15.5 km (9¹/₂ miles)	Loop trip • 29 km (18 miles)
Hiking time • 5 hours	Hiking time • 2–3 days
High point • 1544 m (5900 feet)	High point • 2210 m (7250 feet)
Elevation gain • 299 m (980 feet)	Elevation gain • 914 m (3000 feet)

RESOURCES

Hikable • mid-July to mid-October

Management • Yoho National Park

Topographical maps • Lake Louise 82 N/8, Hector Lake 82 N/9, Blaeberry River 82 N/10

Hiker maps • Topo map available covering the entire park as well as free park trail map

Information • Superintendent, Yoho National Park, Box 99, Field, British Columbia V0A 1G0; phone (604) 343-6433

Permits • Required for overnight hikes

Protection status • Yoho National Park

Our personal list of the most memorable hikes in the Canadian Rockies has the Little Yoho River Valley near the top. Thundering waterfalls, thrusting peaks, mountains, forests, meadows, snowfields, and glaciers. What more could a person ask on so short and easy a walk as the sampler to Twin Falls? Backpackers continue to spectacular views in the high country, choosing from five backcountry campsites; only animals and solitude are lacking for the full six tests for greatness. (Note about the solitude factor: Campsites are nearly always full; make your reservations well in advance.)

Drive east from Field 3.7 km (2.3 miles) on Highway 1 and turn left (north) at the Yoho Valley–Takakkaw Falls exit. The road ends in 13.2 km (8.2 miles) at a walk-in campground, 1518 m (4980 feet). Be sure to park in the correct lot—day or overnight.

Both the day hike and backpack start together from the upper parking lot on the Little Yoho Valley Trail, the first part on an abandoned road through the Takakkaw

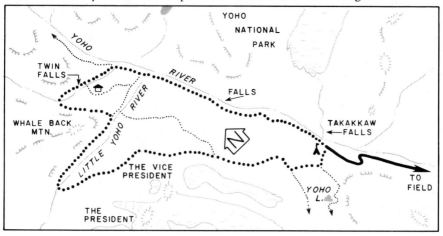

Yoho Glacier from the Whaleback

Falls walk-in campground. Upvalley at 2.7 km the road ends; here are two short, must-do sidetrips, to Angel's Staircase Falls and Point Lace Falls.

Pass a backcountry campsite just below Laughing Falls, 4.8 km, and cross the Little Yoho River. At a split in the trail, continue straight to the next forking at 6.5 km. The right continues 2.4 km upvalley to a viewpoint of Yoho Glacier; go left and climb 1.6 km to a major junction. The left is Twin Falls Chalet, offering lunch and hot drinks and a not-to-be-missed view of the Twin Falls. Day-hikers can loop back home on the Marpole Lake Trail, and then descend left to Laughing Falls and finally down the valley to the trailhead.

Loopers stay right at the Twin Falls junction on the Whaleback Trail, a steady climb to the top of Twin Falls and a backcountry campsite, 1905 m. The way crosses Twin Falls Creek and traverses south over a shoulder of Whaleback Mountain to some of the best views of the trip.

Drop steeply to a major intersection at 13 km and turn right up the Little Yoho River to Little Yoho Campsite at 19 km. Round the Little Yoho Valley and traverse slopes of the Presidential Range over moraines and through meadows to the Celeste Lake Trail, 24 km. Turn right on the Ice Land Trail beside the Emerald Glacier to a junction with the Yoho Lake trail, at 26.8 km, and descend 2.2 km to Whiskey-Jack Youth Hostel. To close the loop, walk the main road back up the valley 1 km to the parking lot.

50 ▪ Lake O'Hara

DAY HIKES
Four from Lake O'Hara basecamp

BACKPACK OR BY BUS
Lake O'Hara by foot
Round trip • 35 km (18 miles)
Hiking time • 4 days
High point • 2408 m (7800 feet)
Elevation gain • 1320 m (4300 feet)
Hikable • late June through September

RESOURCES

Management • Yoho National Park
Topographical map • Lake Louise
Hiker map • Yoho Hikers Map
Information • Yoho National Park, Box 99, Field, British Columbia V0A 1G0; phone
(604) 343-6433
Protection status • Yoho National Park

A blue-green jewel set in high meadows ringed by mountains and sprinkled with many more lakes. The Canadian Rockies, of course, have many such jewels; this one is unique for being accessible by a 16-km (10-mile) bus ride into what otherwise would be wilderness. Without the bus there might be some solitude and wildlife; as it is the visitor must settle for three of the six qualities for greatness, since forests also are meager. A basecamp at the end of the bus road serves days of easy hikes around Lake O'Hara, located below the stark cliffs on the southwest side of Mt. Victoria, the ice-plastered mountain that dominates the view from Lake Louise.

To stay at Lake O'Hara Lodge, the campground, or the Alpine Club of Canada's hut, and to ride the concessionaire's bus, requires reservations. Except for the lodge, arrange for these at the Information Centre in the town of Field, either in person or phone (609) 343-6433. For the lodge, phone (609) 343-6418.

Drive Highway 1 between Lake Louise and Golden. Approximately 3 km (1.8 miles)

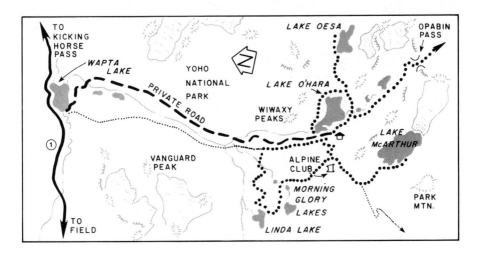

Lake Oesa

west of Kicking Horse Pass, find the Lake O'Hara parking lot and bus terminal, elevation 1600 m (5200 feet). The bus is not compulsory—a delightful trail goes 12 km to the lake along Cataract Brook, gaining 381 m. Inasmuch as the hike fails to provide the proper reward of a wilderness experience, most folks take the bus and save their energy for trips that get away from roads in the high country. Five day hikes, none over 9.6 km, do so very nicely.

Lake Oesa–Wiwaxy Peaks Loop
Loop trip • 8 km (5 miles)
Elevation gain • 496 m (1630 feet)

A waterfall, deep blue Lake Oesa, and a very difficult loop to the broad views from Wiwaxy Gap. Tread carved from cliffs, with easy ups and downs, circles the north side of Lake O'Hara to Lake Oesa. The return alternative by way of Wiwaxy Gap is too steep and mean for most tastes.

Opabin Plateau Circuit
Loop trip • 5.5 km (3 miles)
Elevation gain • 252 m (826 feet)

A pleasant flower walk from the south side of Lake O'Hara to a string of four little lakes. The Highline Scenic Route offers an alternative—and difficult—return by way of Lake Oesa.

Lake McArthur
Round trip • 8 km (5 miles)
Elevation gain • 246 m (810 feet)

A trail on the south side of Lake O'Hara leads to the largest lake in the area. Surrounded by mountains and fed by glaciers, it is also and very definitely the most dramatic.

Linda Lake Loop
Loop trip • 9.5 km (6 miles)
Elevation gain • 244 m (800 feet)

From a start in the Lake O'Hara Campground the trail ambles easily through forest to sparkling clear water of Linda Lake. Continue to more lakes in the Duchesnay Basin. Do more exploring on a primitive trail to Cathedral Basin. If desired, return by way of Odaray Plateau.

Marmot along Lake Oesa trail

51 ▪ Nigel Pass– Brazeau Lake Loop

DAY HIKE
Nigel Pass
Round trip • 16 km (10 miles)
Hiking time • 5 hours
High point • 2208 m (7200 feet)
Elevation gain • 368 m (1200 feet)
Hikable • June through September
Map • NTS Columbia Icefield 83 C/3

BACKPACK
Brazeau Lake Loop
Round trip • 71.2 km (44 miles)
Hiking time • 4–6 days
High point • 2460 m (8069 feet)
Elevation gain • 1970 m (6463 feet)
Hikable • August through September
Maps • NTS Columbia Icefield 83 C/3,
    Sunwapta Peak 83 C/6

RESOURCES
Management • Jasper and Banff National
    Parks
Hiker map • Jasper National Park topo
Information • Superintendent, Jasper
    National Park, P.O. Box 10, Jasper,
    Alberta T0E 1E0; phone (403)
    852-6161
Permits • Required for overnight hikes
Protection status • Jasper and Banff
    National Parks

Just about all the superlatives ever used to describe the alpine scene could be employed here. A day-hike sampler to the high, open meadows of Nigel Pass, the trail well graded and easy, gives views of the sprawling Columbia Icefield and the massive surrounding peaks. However, to get to know this magical land as you must want to do, descend the north side of Nigel Pass to the Brazeau River, on a loop that includes Poboktan and Jonas Passes as well as glacier-fed Brazeau River and tranquil Brazeau Lake. This route requires considerable backpacking experience, routefinding skills, and endurance. It is recommended only in August and September, when the bridgeless creeks are safe to ford and the trails are relatively dry.

At the Banff–Jasper Parks boundary at Sunwapta Pass drive south on Highway 93 for 8 km (5 miles), turn left (northeast) on a gravel road, and park along the edge, taking care not to block the gated service road, 1829 m (6000 feet).

Walk the gravel road 90 m to find the trailhead on the right. The way begins by crossing Nigel Creek and gently ascending the east side of the valley, paralleling the

Nigel Pass

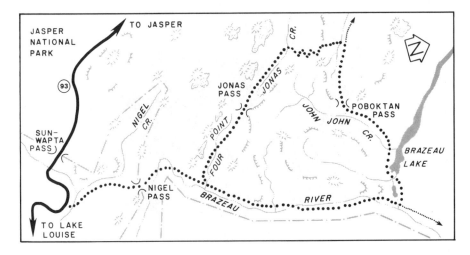

creek. The first campsite at 5.6 km is perched on a sloping hillside of subalpine scrub. Obviously the best is yet to come.

The trail soon enters meadows with views of glaciers and peaks that become more distracting with each step. At 8 km is the 2208-m summit of Nigel Pass, where day-hikers may wander west or east to enticing lakes, or even to the nearby icefields, before heading back down.

Loopers descend north from the pass to follow the Brazeau River, traversing big meadows and twice crossing the river. The Boulder Creek backcountry camp is just beyond the second crossing, 10.3 km. Reach Four Point backcountry campsite, 1919 m, warden's cabin, trail intersection, and the start of the loop portion of the hike at 14.3 km from Highway 93.

Continue down the Brazeau River valley, descending gradually, pleasantly, and easily in open forest and meadows with views of the river and surrounding peaks. Pass a backcountry campsite at 6.4 km from the Four Point junction and a second riverside campsite and warden's cabin at 15.5 km. Beyond the second camp the trail crosses outflow from Brazeau Lake to a major trail intersection, 1720 m. Here the loop turns left, heading west, up the Poboktan Pass trail. Straight ahead is the South Boundary Trail, which goes 150 km north to Medicine Lake.

The trail gently climbs 2 km from the Brazeau River junction to Brazeau Lake and a lakeshore camp area. At 10 km above the Brazeau River junction pass scenic John-John backcountry camp. Poboktan Pass, 2304 m, is crossed at 14.2 km. Descending from the pass the trail crosses and recrosses Poboktan Creek several times. No bridges here, so stay on the northeast side of the creek and make your own way through the tundra. At 17.2 km intersect the Jonas Pass trail, 2100 m. Plan to spend a night in the campsite located 1 km on down Poboktan Creek; no camping is allowed for the next 19.3 km.

Go left at the Jonas Pass junction and ford the chilly waters of Poboktan Creek. The tread is indistinct; stay left of a small creek until you reach 2400 m, then cross the creek and climb to Jonas Shoulder. Descend to Jonas Creek valley and walk meadows to Jonas Pass, 2300 m. The trail descends to the Four Point junction at 19.3 km from Poboktan Creek. Climb back over Nigel Pass to get home.

Fording small stream

52 • Skyline Trail

DAY HIKE
None

BACKPACK
Skyline Trail
One way • 53 km (33 miles)
Hiking time • 3–4 days
High point • 2530 m (8298 feet)
Elevation gain • 850 m (2788 feet)
Hikable • August through September

RESOURCES

Management • Jasper National Park
Topographical maps • Athabasca Falls 83 C/12, Medicine Lake 83 C/13
Hiker maps • Free handout, Jasper National Park topo map
Information • Superintendent, Jasper National Park, P.O. Box 10, Jasper, Aberta
   T0E 1E0; phone (403) 852-6161
Permits • Required for overnight hikes
Protection status • Jasper National Park

The Skyline Trail is the grandest high alpine traverse in Jasper National Park. Of its 53 km (33 miles), 39 (24) are through meadows and along ridge tops of the Maligne Range. No more than 80 people are allowed on the trail at a time and on weekends this quota is nearly always filled. If you wish to hike on a weekend, make advance reservations.

Quite naturally, most folks do the hike one way only. This entails arrangements to hitch the trailheads together. Easiest is to park the car at the lower trailhead and take the bus (twice daily) to the upper trailhead. Be sure to contact Maligne Tours [phone: (403) 852-3370] ahead of time to let them know you wish their services. Aside from that the route has no inconveniences worse than stretches of boggy trail, unbridged stream crossings, much terrain exposed to sudden blasts of cold storms, mosquitoes; plan your hike for August and carry plenty of extra socks, extra clothes, and bug juice.

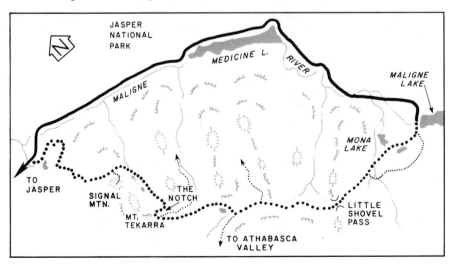

Mount Edith Cavell from Skyline Trail

Drive northeast from the intersection of Highway 93 and Highway 16 (near Jasper townsite) on Highway 16. In 5.9 km (3.7 miles) turn south over a bridge to the Maligne Lake Road. Head up the Maligne River 5.5 km (3.4 miles) to the north or lower trailhead, signed "Northern Terminal Great Divide Trail." Park here and catch the bus for a 36.8-km (23-mile) ride to the road-end parking area at the western tip of Maligne Lake, 1650 m (5414 feet).

From the upper end of the parking lot, the Skyline Trail heads out through lodgepole forest, passing Mona and Lorraine Lakes, crossing Evelyn Creek at 4.4 km, and passing the first of six backcountry camps on the route. The second campsite at 8.4 km is at the forest edge, opening to meadow views that fill the horizons.

Cross Little Shovel Pass, 2225 m, and descend through Snowbowl on a carpet of heather, passing a third camp area. The meadows are soggy and cut by several small streams, at least one of which must be waded. Vegetation gradually dwindles on the ascent to the summit of Big Shovel Pass, 2286 m.

Near the 19.5-km mark the trail divides. The left fork descends by a horse camp to the Athabasca Valley. Skyline Trail stays right, climbing the rocky hillside to Curator Lake and The Notch, 2530 m, the highest elevation of the traverse and offering the biggest views. Snow may linger here all summer.

The trail drops to Tekarra Lake and a backcountry campsite, 2240 m, and traverses around Mt. Tekarra to the Signal Mountain Fire Road. To the left the road climbs a scant 0.5 km to Signal Mountain Lookout, an outstanding viewpoint. The traverse is completed with either an 8.0-km hike down the fire road or via the steep trail that shortcuts the road's switchbacks.

53 ▪ Tonquin Valley

DAY HIKE
None

BACKPACK
Tonquin Valley–Astoria River Trail
Round trip • 36 km (22¹/₂ miles)
Hiking time • 2–3 days
High point • 2118 m (6950 feet)
Elevation gain • 427 m (1400 feet)
Hikable • July to mid-October

RESOURCES

Management • Jasper National Park
Map • NTS Amethyst Lakes 83 D/9
Hiker maps • Jasper National Park topo map, free park trail map
Information • Superintendent, Jasper National Park, P.O. Box 10, Jasper, Alberta
   T0E 1E0; phone (403) 852-6161
Permits • Required for overnight hikes
Protection status • Jasper National Park

Tonquin Valley is a Shangri-La wonderland of meadows and lakes amid rugged mountains. Not surprisingly, it is the most over-loved backcountry of Jasper National Park. To preserve the extremely fragile terrain the number of hikers is limited to sixty per night. During peak season reservations must be made early.

The major problem confronting hikers setting out for the valley is deciding between the two popular accesses. The Astoria River trail is the shortest, has the least elevation gain, and is drier and opens earlier in the summer. The Maccarib Pass trail is far more scenic. The best plan, if transportation can be arranged, is to enter one way and exit the other.

Via Astoria River Trail, drive Highway 93 south from the junction of Highway 93 and Highway 16 near Jasper townsite. In 7 km (4.3 miles) turn right on Highway 93A for 5.2 km (3.2 miles). Turn right on Edith Cavell Road 12.3 km (7.7 miles) and

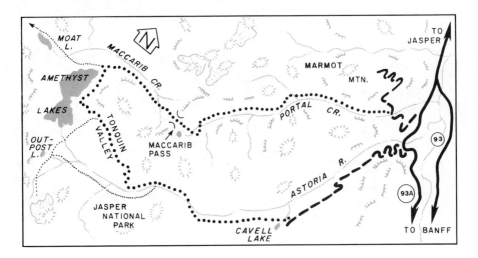

go past the youth hostel to the trailhead parking area, on the right, elevation 1737 m (5700 feet).

The trail is well marked, all major intersections signed, and all creeks bridged. The first campsite is at 7.2 km, just before the Chrome Lake trail junction. Stay right here and switchback out of the valley. At 13.5 km is Switchback Backcountry Camp, the start of meadows and outstanding views. A trail branches left at 15.4 km to Clitheroe Backcountry Camp, Chrome Lake, Outpost Lake, and the Eremite Valley. The highlight of your hike is at 18 km when you set your pack down on a lakeshore campsite at Amethyst Lakes, 2110 m. Two or more days can be spent exploring the valley. Be sure to take in Moat and Outpost Lakes and spend some time just soaking in scenery.

Via Maccarib Pass, following the directions above, turn off Highway 93 onto Highway 93A. Drive 2.4 km (1.5 miles) and turn right on the Marmot Basin Ski Area road 5.8 km (3.6 miles) to Portal Creek. Park on the left side of the road near the horse corral, elevation 1520 m (4987 feet).

From the far end of the parking area the trail sets out up Portal Creek, at 0.5 km crossing to the north side and remaining there the next 7.1 km to Portal Creek Backcountry Camp. The scenery is excellent and continues to improve on the climb to Maccarib Pass, 2210 m, and the descent to Amethyst Lakes. At the north end of the lakes the trail splits. The right fork goes west to Moat Lake and Tonquin Pass; take the left along the lakeshore to Amethyst Lakes Backcountry Campsite, 22 km.

Meadows near Moat Lake

54 ▪ North Boundary Trail

DAY HIKE
None

BACKPACK
North Boundary Trail
One way • 185 km (114³/₄ miles)
Hiking time • 10–14 days
High point • 2019 m (6625 feet)
Elevation gain • 1006 m (3300 feet)

RESOURCES

Hikable • mid-July to September
Management • Jasper National Park
Maps • NTS Snaring 83 E/1, Rock Lake 83 E/8, Blue Creek 83 E/7 E and W,
   Twintree Lake 83 E/6 E and W, Mt. Robson 83 E/3
Hiker map • Jasper National Park topo
Information • Superintendent, Jasper National Park and Mt. Robson Provincial Park,
   P.O. Box 10, Jasper, Alberta T0E 1E0; phone (403) 852-6161
Permits • Required
Protection status • Jasper National Park

Jasper National Park maintains two lengthy backcountry routes exclusively for hikers and horse-riders. The South Boundary Trail starts near Medicine Lake and ends 176 km (110 miles) south, beyond Nigel Pass (see Hike 51). The North Boundary Trail is the more scenic. The forests and solitude make this a great; if the full route is hiked there also are views and meadows—and wildlife such as is offered by few other trails. Normally it is hiked from its east end in the Athabasca River valley to its west terminus in Mount Robson Provincial Park, the scene gradually changing from forest to the high alpine grandeur of Berg Lake. Great though the trek absolutely is, to enjoy it a person

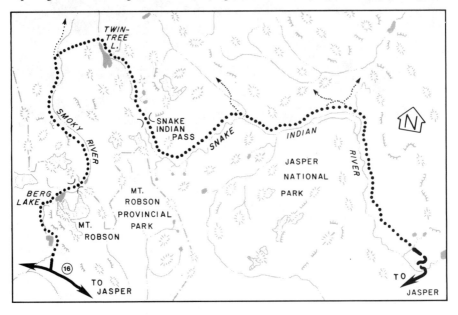

Eastern end of North Boundary Trail

must have the proper mind-set. The route does not consist solely of high alpine passes and shining lakes that keep a camera clicking and whirring. There are those in glorious abundance, but they lie in a setting of *complete* wilderness, which by definition includes miles of valley bottoms that a "high-grading" wilderness visitor might call tedious. One factor that helps keep up interest is that the hiker shares the trail with more deer, moose, caribou, bear, and wolves than humans. The occasional stream, bridgeless and rushing, also adds excitement.

The start is the hardest part. If two vehicles are available one can be left at each end. With just one, it is best to leave it at the Berg Lake trailhead in Mount Robson

Provincial Park and catch the bus to Jasper townsite, where hikers must arrange for backcountry permits at the Park Visitors Information Centre. Now comes the tricky bit—getting to the trailhead. Head east on Highway 16 for 13 km (8.1 miles) to the Celestine Lake Road. (This demands ingenuity if you don't have a second car. Try hiring a taxi or hitching a ride.) Go left 5 km (3 miles) to the Snaring Campground registration booth and (if driving) check on the condition of the road ahead. Drive or walk 1.3 km (0.8 mile) to the end of pavement and the beginning of one-way road. If driving, obey the time schedule (available at the information centre) and continue for 26.6 km (16.5 miles) on very rough road to the Celestine Lake parking lot, elevation 1200 m (4100 feet). If afoot you'll find campsites along the road. However, if walking the road be sure to add an extra day to your itinerary and more food.

The North Boundary Trail begins on a fire road up the Snake Indian River. Backcountry campsites are spaced at intervals of no more than 14 km; camping is not allowed except at these sites. The mood of the terrain is subdued until Snake Indian Falls, 21 km. The route then leaves the fire road and the scenery intensifies. At 32 km the trail bends west to big views from meadows. At 91 km is the summit of Snake Indian Pass, 2019 m. The trail descends to Twintree Lake, then ascends the Smokey River to high alpine country and Robson Pass at 170 km. The wilderness ends abruptly here as the trail leaves Jasper National Park and enters Mount Robson Provincial Park. Descend past Berg Lake through the Valley of a Thousand Falls (see Hike 55).

Those with the time will find a host of interesting sidetrips from the North Boundary Trail. Rock Creek and Azure Lake are highly recommended. An extra day easily can be spent around Berg Lake.

Bighorn sheep

55 • Berg Lake

DAY HIKE
None

BACKPACK
Berg Lake
Round trip • 35 km (22 miles)
Hiking time • 2–4 days
High point • 1646 m (5400 feet)
Elevation gain • 792 m (2570 feet)

RESOURCES

Hikable • late June to mid-October
Management • Mount Robson Provincial Park
Topographical map • Mt. Robson 83 E/3
Hiker map • Use topographical
Information • Mount Robson Provincial Park, 1101 4th Avenue, Prince George,
    British Columbia V2L 3H9; phone (604) 565-6270; or Mount Robson Visitors
    Centre, open May to September
Permits • Camping permits needed
Protection status • Mount Robson Provincial Park

The names suggest the treasure: Mt. Robson, Emperor Falls, Valley of a Thousand
Falls, and Berg Lake. But the names don't tell that Robson is the highest mountain
in the Canadian Rockies and that Berg Lake is named not for chunks of frozen lake
but because a glacier drops in genuine icebergs. The names also don't mention the ancient
forest at the beginning of the trail or the fields of alpine flowers near Berg Lake. Altogether
this is a classic, even though animals are scarce and people not. Thirty years ago, the
lake was accessible to only the toughest wilderness adventurer, impossible for a mild-
mannered hiker. The installation of footbridges has made it one of the most popular
hikes in the Canadian Rockies, and rightly so.

Drive Highway 16 to between the towns of Cache Creek and Jasper. At Robson
Viewpoint Visitor Centre leave the highway and go north 2.3 km (about 4 miles) to

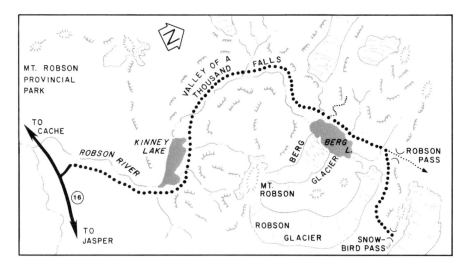

Berg Lake and Mount Robson

the Berg Lake parking area and trailhead, elevation 900 m (2900 feet).

The trail (at the start, an abandoned service road) goes through forest 4.4 km to milky-green Kinney Lake, 984 m. The way rounds the east shore, climbs a bit, and crosses the wide swath of braided channels of Robson River. The channels frequently swap around, washing away bridges, and until the engineers arrive that's it for the hiker.

From the river the trail climbs to the Valley of a Thousands Falls. Is the number really 1000? During early-summer snowmelt there are too many to count. Indeed, at any time of summer hot weather may turn little streams into raging torrents—and no bridges. At 17.5 km is Berg Lake, 1646 m.

Berg Lake is a "far enough" destination where it is sufficient to poke nose from the tent door and be entranced all day. However, hikers whose legs quiver uncontrollably during inactivity may well wish to continue 8–9 km to the super-dramatic views of the icy north side of Robson from Snowbird Pass. Go 2.4 km beyond the lake. Near Robson Pass turn right on a rough, cairn-marked path close to the blue ice of Robson Glacier. At about 7 km from the lake go up a steep, brushy hillside. In meadow above the brush the tread becomes obscure. Simply head for the obvious lowest point in the ridge, Snowbird Pass, 2500 m, overlooking the Coleman Glacier and Reef Icefield. Before the trail was built, this awesome view was known only to semi-expeditionary mountain climbers. That's progress.

Berg Lake trail

Index

THE MOUNTAINEERS, founded in 1906, is a non-profit outdoor activity and conservation club, whose mission is "to explore, study, preserve and enjoy the natural beauty of the outdoors. . . ." Based in Seattle, Washington, the club is now the third largest such organization in the United States, with 12,000 members and four branches throughout Washington State.

The Mountaineers sponsors both classes and year-round outdoor activities in the Pacific Northwest, which include hiking, mountain climbing, ski-touring, snowshoeing, bicycling, camping, kayaking and canoeing, nature study, sailing, and adventure travel. The club's conservation division supports environmental causes through educational activities, sponsoring legislation, and presenting informational programs. All club activities are led by skilled, experienced volunteers, who are dedicated to promoting safe and responsible enjoyment and preservation of the outdoors.

The Mountaineers Books, an active, non-profit publishing program of the club, produces guidebooks, instructional texts, historical works, natural history guides, and works on environmental conservation. All books produced by The Mountaineers are aimed at fulfilling the club's mission.

If you would like to participate in these organized outdoor activities or the club's programs, consider a membership in The Mountaineers. For information and an application, write or call The Mountaineers, Club Headquarters, 300 Third Avenue West, Seattle, Washington 98119; (206) 284-6310.

FOOTSORE Series
Harvey Manning. Highly personal guides to year-round walks and hikes near cities around Puget Sound.
- 1: Seattle, Issaquah Alps
- 3: Everett to Bellingham
- 4: Puyallup, Nisqually, Kitsap

EXPLORING OREGON'S WILD AREAS:
A Guide for Hikers, Backpackers, XC Skiers & Paddlers
William L. Sullivan. Detail-stuffed guidebook to Oregon's wilderness areas, wildlife refuges, nature preserves, and state parks.

EXPLORING IDAHO'S MOUNTAINS: A Guide for Climbers, Scramblers, and Hikers
Tom Lopez. Route directions and descriptions for more than 700 summits in Idaho. Includes elevation gain, summit elevation, difficulty, information on geology, weather, mountain names, addresses for more details.

ADVENTURES IN IDAHO'S SAWTOOTH COUNTRY:
63 Trips for Hikers & Mountain Bikers
Lynne Stone. Where-tos and how-tos for hiking and biking trails near Sun Valley, Ketchum, Hailey, and Stanley area. Includes designation, distance, duration, elevation gain, and more.

FIELD GUIDE TO THE CASCADES & OLYMPICS
Stephen R. Whitney. Describes and beautifully illustrates more than 600 species of plants and animals found in mountains from Northern California through Southwest British Columbia.

MOUNTAIN FLOWERS
Ira Spring, Harvey Manning. Full-color photos and descriptions of 84 of the most common wildflowers in the Cascade and Olympic mountain ranges.

MOUNTAINEERING: The Freedom of the Hills, 5th Ed.
Don Graydon, editor. Complete instruction on how to climb: ropes, knots, belaying, rappelling; rock, snow, ice climbing; wilderness navigation.

MEDICINE FOR MOUNTAINEERING
James Wilkerson, M.D., editor. The "bible" of wilderness medicine for back-country travelers or expeditions more than 24 hours away from medical aid.

MOUNTAINEERING FIRST AID
Martha J. Lentz, Steven C. MacDonald, Jan Carline. Fully updated, basic outdoor first aid; conforms to latest mountaineering-oriented first aid classes.

Send for illustrated catalog of more than 200 outdoor books published by:
The Mountaineers
1011 S.W. Klickitat Way, Suite 107
Seattle, WA 98134